NAME:

_____

START DATE:

_____

END DATE:

_____

DEVOTIONAL GUIDE

WHATEVER IS

TRUE & LOVELY

CARRIE CRISTANCHO

DaySpring
LIVE YOUR FAITH

A Note From the Author

I didn't actually know the Bible until a few years ago. I know that seems like a terrible way to start a devotional guide, but stick with me. I grew up in a Christian home, and I learned all the stories. I knew the books of the Bible in their order by the time I was six, and I have so many verses committed to memory I could probably quote a verse for any occasion. I knew the gospel, and I understood that I was a sinner and that Jesus died in my place. But that was pretty much where my biblical literacy (or knowledge of the Bible) ended. Until a few years ago, I didn't know that the Bible was one story. I always thought it was a bunch of books without any rhyme or reason to them. I didn't know the journey of Israel, and I didn't really understand why we needed Jesus other than being sinners. When I started to read the Bible for real, I learned that the Bible wasn't just Sunday school stories. The Bible is truth. It's history. It's the Word of God. Learning its

overarching narrative helped me realize that this book wasn't just something to read on Sundays but something to be studied every day. It's something to live by.

Then I started reading the Bible with the intention of studying it. In order to keep track of my thoughts, I decided to create an Instagram account. I posted photos of my Bible with detailed thoughts in the captions. I wanted to come up with a social media handle that would remind me of why I was studying the Word. I began this journey in Philippians and thought of Philippians 4:8 (CSB): Finally, brothers and sisters, whatever is true, whatever is honorable, whatever is just, whatever is pure, whatever is lovely, whatever is commendable—if there is any moral excellence and if there is anything praiseworthy—dwell on these things.

There was no better way to remind myself of why I cared about studying the Bible than a verse about how to be like Jesus, so I called my account True and Lovely Words. Since then, God has done huge things. At the end of my first year, I started offering different Bible study resources, the next year I started a blog with more in-depth writing, and in the year after that, I started a podcast. True and Lovely Words became True and Lovely Co., and beyond the growth in my audience and platforms, my love for the Lord and His Word has grown even more.

I am so passionate about the Bible—I'm a self-proclaimed Bible nerd. Finding connections within the text is one of my favorite things in the whole world, and I could talk about Scripture for hours. It's one thing to know Scripture; it's another to practice it. James tells us not to be just hearers of the Word but doers, but it can be hard to know where to start! There are some days when I just don't know how to handle a situation or circumstance, and I want to get angry. But I always go back to Philippians.

As followers of Jesus, our lives can't just be about knowing the gospel—we need to reflect it as well. We do that by dwelling on God's Word and acting in ways that are true and lovely.

WHAT IS THE BIBLE?

- The Bible is a large book comprised of sixty-six smaller books. The Bible is broken down into two parts. The first thirty-nine books are called the Old Testament. It covers the creation of the world and the history of God's chosen people, the Israelites. The last twenty-seven books are called the New Testament. It includes four Gospels that tell the story of the life of Christ; Acts, which gives an overview of the beginning of the church; twenty-one letters, also known as Epistles; and the book of Revelation, a prophetic book about the return of Christ and the end times.

- The Bible is a book about God. If you make the Bible about you, you'll never be satisfied, and it will never truly make sense to you. The first step to properly understand God's Word is making sure you study the Bible to learn more about Him.

- The Bible is the Word of God, and the entire thing points to Christ. In his book *Christian Beliefs,* Wayne Grudem says, "The words of Scripture are more than simply true; they are truth itself." The Bible teaches us how sin came into the world and about the consequences of sin. It teaches us how fickle and shortsighted humans are and how sovereign, gracious, and just the Lord is. It teaches redemption and forgiveness while challenging us to be more like Christ. The Bible's overall theme comes down to one truth: We are sinful, but God is gracious. And out of His grace and love for us, He sent Christ to be the ultimate sacrifice to atone for our sins.

- The Word of God is a well of wisdom that leads us to a life of obedience (Psalm 119:9–11). It is a light in the darkness (Psalm 119:105), and it is hope in affliction (Psalm 119:50). The Bible is history of the world and knowledge from the Creator Himself. It shows us how sinful we are by nature and how much God loves us anyway (Romans 5:8). The Bible is our heavenly Father's way of communicating with us. It "is living and active, sharper than any two-edged sword, piercing to the division of soul and of spirit, of joints and of marrow" (Hebrews 4:12 ESV). The Word of God isn't a bandage for our problems. It's a tool that teaches us about the Lord, describes His goodness throughout history, and refines us to become more like Him.

THE BIBLE IS NOT

- The Bible is not a self-help book. Many people use the Bible as a source of encouragement. This isn't a bad thing. The Word of God is the best place to turn to when we need help, and it's important we take care of ourselves. There is so much encouragement in the Bible, but that's not all there is. Scripture also teaches us how to live so we can bring glory to God.

- The Bible is not a group of fictional stories. As we talked about earlier, the Old Testament is a historical narrative.

- The Bible is also not exclusive to a select few. The Bible exists so that anyone may read it and know God (Psalm 119:130). You don't have to be in Bible college to study the Bible. You don't have to be a pastor or a scholar. The Bible is for everyone, and the only things you need for studying the Bible are your Bible and your brain. There are so many fantastic resources available to help you understand things better, but they aren't a requirement. Everyone can know and study the Bible.

WHY WE STUDY THE BIBLE

- Studying the Bible helps us correctly interpret and apply the Bible. Often, Scripture is taken out of context and applied in a way that isn't at all what the original author intended. It's important that we let Scripture interpret Scripture and consider a verse in light of the verses surrounding it. Application is dependent upon understanding, and if a verse isn't understood correctly, it will likely be applied incorrectly as well.

II TIMOTHY 3:16-17 NIV

"All Scripture is God-breathed and is useful for teaching, rebuking, correcting and training in righteousness, so that the servant of God may be thoroughly equipped for every good work."

"All Scripture is God breathed . . ." The Bible was written by men but inspired by God. The words you read in your Bible are the very words of God. He is in every book and on every page, and He breathed life into every word. If we want to hear from the Lord, we open Scripture.

". . . and is useful for teaching, rebuking, correcting and training in righteousness . . ." Scripture refines us to be more like Christ. Colossians 3:10 says, "[You have] put on the new self, which is being renewed in knowledge after the image of its Creator" (NIV). We are called to reflect Christ, and as imperfect humans, that requires refinement and process. First Timothy 4:7 tells us, "But have nothing to do with pointless and silly myths. Rather, train yourself in godliness" (CSB).

Our ultimate example of godliness is Jesus. How can we train ourselves in godliness if we don't study the life of Jesus, the source of life itself? How can we bear the fruits of the Spirit (Galatians 5:22–23) if we don't first reflect the Spirit?

". . . so that the servant of God may be thoroughly equipped for every good work." Studying the Bible gives us a solid foundation to stand on in life. No matter the circumstance, the Bible provides us with the wisdom we need to handle any situation. Sometimes it's a practical answer to a question. Other times the Bible guides us on how to handle something when we feel confused about what to do. No matter the situation, the Bible has an answer for it.

At this point, you may be wondering if studying the Bible is worth all the effort. Knowing the Bible is an essential part of bearing fruit and reflecting Christ. When you know the Word, you know your Father. When you hide His Word in your heart, it's far easier to follow it (Psalm 119:11). When you know what the Lord says about certain situations, you can respond in a way that glorifies Him.

How to Study the Bible

First and foremost, let Scripture interpret Scripture.

You will need your Bible. Open it up and read it—for real. Write down questions you have and search for the answers to those questions. Write down your thoughts and prayers about a passage in a notebook or in the margins of your Bible. You may get through a few chapters a day; you may only get through a few verses in a day. You may end up going on a treasure hunt as you bounce from reference to reference. There is no minimum number of verses or chapters you must read every day to study the Bible correctly; it's about your intention.

Studying the Bible isn't something you do passively. You won't always learn things quickly, and you will almost certainly misunderstand things. Guess what? It's okay. Don't let these temporary setbacks get in your way. Press on! It's okay to have questions. Thankfully, there are many resources available that give you the ability to dig deeper, find answers, and "check your work," for lack of a better term.

Commentaries, concordances, dictionaries, and references—oh my! These are fantastic tools to help you understand the Bible, the culture of the time, and so much more. Let's talk about each of these helpful tools and how they might fit in to your study time.

Translations—The first, and often easiest, way to get a richer understanding of Scripture is to read a portion of the text in different translations. Different translations of a text will have the same core meaning, but the translation to English may be different based on a variety of things. It's important to note that the core message of the Bible does not change based on translation. I could honestly write pages on translations and the differences between them but, in short, different translations have interpreted the original manuscripts differently. You'll see I've used a variety of translations in this devotional guide—the Christian Standard Bible (CSB), alongside the New International Version (NIV), the English Standard Version (ESV), and the New King James Version (NKJV).

References/Cross-references—Found in a Bible or online or in a concordance, references/cross-references are used to see where something is found in Scripture. For example, a verse that mentions "grace by faith" has multiple cross-references, which are other verses about grace by faith. These are important to study because Scripture interprets Scripture. A cross-reference of a verse may have more information than the original verse and can help us understand an idea more fully.

Concordances—These are similar to cross-references but are on a broader scale. You can usually find a concordance in the back of your Bible, and there are many online. These resources tell you how often a specific word or phrase is used in the Bible and where to find it. Concordances don't take context into account when listing verses, so you can't always use them to relate two verses or passages, but they are very helpful if you're researching a specific topic.

Interlinear concordances—This is where things get super fun! Concordances give us a list of references that mention a particular word. Interlinear concordances do the same thing but with the original text. The Bible was written in mostly Greek (New Testament) and Hebrew/Aramaic (Old Testament). Interlinear concordances give you the ability to see the original word and see where else it is in the Bible. This matters because while the Bible has been translated over the years, it's helpful to see how and where specific words were used to better understand the text we're studying.

Commentaries—Commentaries are texts that explain Scripture. They can be incredibly helpful when studying the Bible, but I always recommend them as a secondary source of clarification since they are human interpretations of Scripture. Many of them are theologically sound, but we still need to dig into Scripture to understand it for ourselves before we examine commentaries. When it comes to commentaries, make sure whoever wrote or contributed to the one you choose has solid theology and focuses on the text rather than how it makes the author feel. I find it most helpful to use these last to "check my work" rather than using them as my source of interpretation. Once you break down a passage for yourself, you can see what other trusted theologians and pastors have said about the passage.

Guides and Studies—Guides, like the one you're reading, and studies can be incredibly useful tools when studying the Bible. They are a great way to help you stay focused and keep track of what you're studying. They don't always give you the answer to a question, but rather point you in the direction of the answer so you can dig into it yourself. There are so many incredible guides and studies out there. When you choose one, I encourage you to make sure it points you to Scripture first!

STEP BY STEP

Starting your Bible study and Bible journaling journey can often be the most challenging part. You may be nervous about writing in your Bible or unsure where to start, and that's okay! The goal is to know the Bible. The creative or in-Bible journaling part comes later. Remember, the cover, binding, and pages of the book itself are not our priority. The goal is learning the Word of God to understand how to reflect Christ for His glory.

There are some specific steps to studying the Bible that can improve your biblical literacy. You may find that changing up the order of these steps works better for you. You may spend more time on a particular step than others. You may end up combining steps as you start to develop a routine. All of this is okay! The exercises in this book are meant to give you a starting point so you can develop the skills to study and understand the Bible.

Step 1: Prayer

When you begin with prayer, you recognize the Author of the Bible and spend some time talking with Him before starting your study. Share with Him any distractions you may be facing or any sin you're struggling with. Pray about your study. Pray that He would reveal Himself through

His Word. If you're struggling with what to pray about, start with gratitude and worship. Acknowledge who He is and all He has done. Whether you journal your prayer, pray out loud, or pray quietly to yourself, take a few minutes to invite the Holy Spirit into your study time.

Step 2: Read and Identify

After prayerfully choosing the passage you'll study, read it through once or twice to get a basic understanding of what it's saying. Jot down things that stand out to you or confuse you. Don't look too far into the passage yet! This is a general review of the text. Personally, I like to jot down things that catch my attention, things I want to make a note about, and things that are confusing to me at first glance.

Step 3: Context and Understanding

Here's where it gets fun! It's important to relate what you read to the original audience so you can understand a passage's meaning. To do this, answer these questions:

- Who is the author of this passage?
- Who is the audience?
- How do you think this passage impacted the audience?

Remember: The Bible isn't about us. It's about God. If we try to apply everything to our own lives, we'll miss the message. If we apply everything to the Lord and try to learn something about Him, we'll find it. As a starting point to get my mind ready for the text, I often ask myself: Where do I see the Lord? His provision? A characteristic such as love or sovereignty? You can do the same. Go through the text and see what it says about the Lord.

Key themes are things or messages you frequently see throughout a passage. It's easier to find them in some books and harder in others. When looking for key themes, look for phrases that repeat or a larger idea that weaves through a portion of Scripture (examples include grace, love, mercy, blessing, covenant, judgment, etc.).

If you're unsure how to answer these questions based on the passage alone, that's okay! This is where the rubber meets the road. You may need to look at a different chapter of the book to find the audience. If you're reading a letter, who wrote it and who received it? If you're reading a historical book like Genesis or I Samuel, see if any references in your Bible give you clues to its author. If you get stuck and can't find the answer, then use the resources we talked about earlier.

Tip: Don't start off looking at the notes in your study Bible! Try to find the answers yourself. It is so much more fruitful and rewarding!

Step 4: Application

This step requires proper interpretation (from step 2), personal responsibility, and discernment. Not every passage in Scripture will apply directly to us. Application comes after interpretation because it's critical to have the correct interpretation of the text before applying it to our lives. Make sure you don't look past the passages that convict or refine you! God is good, and each of us will always be a work in progress. If a portion of text doesn't apply to you in your current season, reflect on how you can respond to the Lord as a result of what you've learned.

Step 5: Write It in Your Bible

If you're the type of person who wants to write everything in your Bible, go for it! There's no wrong way to do that. If you want to write less or nothing in your Bible, that's okay too. As you gain more knowledge and understanding, you can journal, draw, paint, or color in your pages. Maybe you'll want to put important notes in the margins next to passages that really speak to you. Perhaps you'll want to put quotes, prayers, or other verses next to the text. Again, there is no right or wrong way to do this. Just enjoy the process.

Bible Journaling and What You Need

Bible journaling is a popular way to study the Word. For some, Bible journaling means drawing, painting, lettering, and even scrapbook-type journaling. For others, like myself, Bible journaling is more writing and note-taking. Neither style is better than the other; they're just different.

Bible journaling is a useful tool for many people because it can bring a creative element to Bible study. For me, I can't just read something and retain information. I need to write it down. Some people like to paint or draw to better retain information. At its core, the point of Bible journaling is to study the Word of God and be able to accurately apply it to our lives. It connects us with the text and keeps us focused and engaged in our study.

Remember, journaling is a form of worship and a method for refinement, not for aesthetics. Bible journaling is a way to encourage biblical study and literacy, not a way to show off artistic talent on its own. If you're more focused on how it looks than what and—more importantly—WHO it's about, I encourage you to take a step back and reflect on why you're studying Scripture. I have to do this often with the platform I have, and it's such an important part of Bible journaling. Your journaling method is yours! Go with whatever helps you best understand and apply the text to your life so you can honor the Lord and reflect Christ.

SUPPLIES:

The only things you need to Bible journal are a Bible and something to write with.

Here is something that is nice to have:

Journaling Bible

These are different from your standard Bible. Journaling Bibles (or Note-taking Bibles as some are called) have a wide margin that often have lines for note-taking. There are so many options! Some Bibles have lined margins; some have blank margins. As you read through Scripture in this guide, you'll notice both! If you're someone who writes a lot or wants extra room for art-style journaling, *The Illustrating Bible* from DaySpring has huge margins that make Bible journaling a dream!

Another version of a Bible that will give you room to write is called an interleaved Bible. These are big Bibles, but they have a blank page, front and back, between every page, which gives a ton of room. But you don't technically need a journaling Bible or an interleaved Bible to study the Bible. I promise!

Here are some of the things I recommend having:

Pens

Ballpoint pens tend to be the easiest to use in your Bible because they rarely show through on the other side. Most Bibles have very thin pages, and you'll have to decide whether you're more bothered by seeing a "ghost" of the ink from a fineliner or gel pen on the other side of the paper or by indenting the paper as you write with a ballpoint pen. Ballpoint pens also tend to be less expensive, while fineliner style pens often have more color options.

Highlighters

There are so many kinds, and everyone has a personal preference. I find the lighter Zebra Mildliners and the pastel Tombow Dual Brush Pens work great for me.

Sticky notes or small papers and washi tape

I like using washi tape to adhere my notes to the pages because lighter washi is see-through. You don't need to move the note because you can read underneath it, and if you do need to remove it, it's easier on the paper.

I recommend using some of the last pages of your Bible as a place to test pens and highlighters. Highlight over text, highlight over something you write, scribble, doodle, or whatever you do as you Bible journal. Having these test pages will help you see the performance of your pens and highlighters in your Bible.

As you start to develop your personal style of journaling, you may take away or add items as you like them. In addition to the above, I also always have a Tombow Fudenosuke brush pen handy to letter things that stand out. Of course, how you journal is totally up to you, and as you study the Word, how you journal will likely change and evolve.

MY PRAYER FOR YOU

As we navigate Scripture together
over the next twenty-five days, my prayer is that
you grow in knowledge of God's Word
and in your relationship with Christ.
I pray that you are so intrigued with what
you've learned in the following pages, that
you don't stop digging deep into the Word,
but that you continue to seek the Truth.
Most importantly, I pray that you leave
each day more in love with God and
the Word He's graciously given us.

Sincerely,

DAY 1

Finally brothers and sisters, whatever is true, whatever is honorable, whatever is just, whatever is pure, whatever is lovely, whatever is commendable—if there is any moral excellence and if there is anything praiseworthy—dwell on these things.

PHILIPPIANS 4:8 CSB

Whatever Is True and Lovely

What better way to start out this study than to dig into the passage that started my journey into knowing the Bible. There is so much rich truth in Philippians, and the first nine verses have made a huge impact in my life.

Verses 4–7 remind us of the goodness of God. They remind us that His peace, a peace that we can't understand, will not just come over us but guard our hearts and minds. How amazing is that promise? What is one of my favorite takeaways of these verses? We can bring anything and everything to the Lord—but let's remember to bring them to Him with thanksgiving. He knows our needs. He knows our prayers. It is so hard sometimes, but it's important to remember that the Lord is good and that we have so much to be thankful for. Even in the times that are hard, He will use our circumstance for His glory and that is something to be thankful for!

Verse 8 is one of my all-time favorite verses. It is the foundation of my ministry and a verse I fall back on regularly. One thing about me—I love action plans. I worked for nearly a decade in an industry where process and policy were top priorities. We had action plans for everything. Whenever it seems hard to reflect Christ, I go back to this verse as my policy. What does it look like to be like Jesus? It looks like dwelling on what is true, noble, right, pure, and everything else Paul lists. It's a reminder of how we can practically put into action a reflection of the Lord, and I think that's such a wonderful reminder to have.

Philippians 4:13 is one of the most commonly quoted verses in the Bible. It's a verse of encouragement and promise. It's so important, however, to interpret it correctly. As you work through the study questions, here are a few things to consider:

- Paul was in prison when he wrote the book of Philippians. You'd never know it based on his writing, but he was imprisoned in Rome and writing to the church at Philippi because he was thankful for their support.

- We often use this verse as a motivator for events or things we hope will go our way, but focus on verses 11 and 12. How do you see verse 13 differently in light of his circumstance and what he writes here?

After you read this passage and go through today's study, I encourage you to set aside half an hour to read the book of Philippians. Even if you don't study it in depth today, reading the whole book knowing Paul's circumstance when he wrote it will help you see this letter in a new way.

Philippians 4:4–13

WHATEVER IS TRUE
AND LOVELY

Rejoice in the Lord always. I will say it again: Rejoice! Let your graciousness be known to everyone. The Lord is near. Don't worry about anything, but in everything, through prayer and petition with thanksgiving, present your requests to God. And the peace of God, which surpasses all understanding, will guard your hearts and minds in Christ Jesus. Finally brothers and sisters, whatever is true, whatever is honorable, whatever is just, whatever is pure, whatever is lovely, whatever is commendable—if there is any moral excellence and if there is anything praiseworthy—

dwell on these things. Do what you have learned and received and heard from me, and seen in me, and the God of peace will be with you. I rejoiced in the Lord greatly because once again you renewed your care for me. You were, in fact, concerned about me but lacked the opportunity to show it. I don't say this out of need, for I have learned to be content in whatever circumstances I find myself. I know how to make do with little, and I know how to make do with a lot. In any and all circumstances I have learned the secret of being content—whether well fed or hungry, whether in abundance or in need. I am able to do all things through him who strengthens me.

Reflect

Who is the author of this passage? Who is the audience?

How do you think this passage impacted the audience?

Reflect

What do you see about the Lord?

What key themes do you see?

Verse Breakdown

Tells us this is the last statement of the passage - a reminder to read prior verses for context

Tells us who the author is talking to - in this case, Paul's brothers & sisters in Christ in Philippi

These are not just bullet point attributes we should pursue for ourselves - They are also attributes of God.

"**Finally**, **brothers and sisters**, whatever is **true**, whatever is **noble**, whatever is **right**, whatever is **pure**, whatever is **lovely**, whatever is **admirable**—if anything is **excellent** or **praiseworthy**—think about such things."

Philippians 4:8
NIV

Call to action. Think, meditate on, & be in pursuit of these things.

We should aim to reflect Him in our lives - these characteristics are a straight-forward starting point.

attributes that reflect the Lord

In light of what you learned and observed, how can you apply this to your life and/or how should you respond to the Lord?

_____
_____
_____
_____
_____
_____

Other Scriptures to consider
JOHN 3:16 | PSALM 23 | 2 TIMOTHY 3:16–17

DAY 2

All Scripture is God-breathed and is useful for teaching, rebuking, correcting and training in righteousness, so that the servant of God may be thoroughly equipped for every good work.

II TIMOTHY 3:16–17 NIV

The Very Words of God

As we continue digging into Scripture, let's set a foundation for what the Bible is. We talked about this at the beginning of the guide, but let's get into it for ourselves over the next few pages. Verse 16 in II Timothy 3 tells us that Scripture is "God-breathed"; this appears as "inspired by God" in other translations of Scripture. We are blessed to have access to the actual Word of God! We can connect with Him through His Word whenever we want. We can learn about the overall narrative of the Bible, we can study the gospel, and we can grow Lord closer to Him through His own words. God breathed life into creation, and He breathed life into the Words of Scripture—what a beautiful concept!

When I first studied the Bible, I went in hoping to get something out of it every single time. Unfortunately, I set myself up for failure because I was looking for the Bible to tell me something about myself and my circumstances. Instead of seeing the Bible as a book about God and my response to Him, I saw the Bible as something that needed to serve me. I often come back to this passage in Paul's letter to Timothy because I think it's a great reminder of how to approach the Bible.

God's Word is absolutely encouraging. It's filled with love, grace, joy, and hope. We do ourselves such a disservice when we see it as only that, though. It is God's Word, intended to teach us about Him, correct us to be more like Him, and equip us for the work He has for us. How incredible is it that the God who created the universe also made His Word available to us so that we can do everything He's called us to do? His Word is such a gift!

As we spend the next few weeks together digging into His Word, my prayer is that you will see how incredible and special the Bible's words are.

Verse Breakdown

Your turn! Turn the page and use the margins provided to break down Scripture for yourself.

Once you've completed the "Reflect" section, come back and make a note of how you can apply this Scripture to your life and/or how you should respond to the Lord in light of what you've observed.

II Timothy 3:10–17 (NIV)
THE VERY WORDS OF GOD

You, however, know all about my teaching, my way of life, my purpose, faith, patience, love, endurance, persecutions, sufferings—what kinds of things happened to me in Antioch, Iconium and Lystra, the persecutions I endured. Yet the Lord rescued me from all of them. In fact, everyone who wants to live a godly life in Christ Jesus will be persecuted, while evildoers and impostors will go from bad to worse, deceiving and being deceived. But as for you, continue in what you have learned and have become convinced of, because you know those from whom you learned it, and how from infancy you have known the Holy Scriptures, which are able to make you wise for salvation through faith in Christ Jesus. All Scripture is God-breathed and is useful for teaching, rebuking, correcting and training in righteousness, so that the servant of God may be thoroughly equipped for every good work.

> **Other Scriptures to consider**
> *JOHN 1:1–5 | HEBREWS 4:12 | PSALM 19:7–8*

Reflect

Who is the author of this passage? Who is the audience?

How do you think this passage impacted the audience?

Reflect

What do you see about the Lord?

What key themes do you see?

DAY 3

Set your minds on things above, not on earthly things.

COLOSSIANS 3:2 NIV

Eternal Over Earthly

There are two things written in my Bible more than anything else: "God is sovereign" and "eternal over earthly." These are themes we will see often while studying God's Word. It's easy to say we will focus on what is eternal instead of what is earthly, but in the thick of life, it's hard to put into practice. We are surrounded by a godless culture and what the world deems worthy. It's easy to get pulled in to worldliness. The battle between the world and what is godly has existed since the fall of humanity (Genesis 3), and thankfully, the Bible gives us so much encouragement for how to navigate through this conflict.

When Paul wrote to the church in Colossae, they were struggling with the same issues. One thing that stands out to me in this passage is the list of what is earthly. Paul starts by mentioning the obvious ones—evil desires, sexual immorality, and others we easily connect to being sinful. He then follows up with a list of things that are sometimes glorified in culture: anger, slander, and filthy language. Being hotheaded is sometimes an acceptable character trait today, and cursing and using other foul language are widely accepted. None of these things glorify God, and I love Paul's boldness to include those "more acceptable" sins with the obvious ones.

Another thing that stands out is Paul's explanation of why we ought to seek what is eternal over what is earthly. When we accept Jesus as our Savior and choose to follow Him, our lives before Him are "hidden with Christ in God" (Colossians 3:3 CSB). Before Jesus, our lives were sinful and full of the world. Jesus defeated sin and death, allowing us to live in His victory. We are redeemed, our sins are forgotten, and as a result, let's focus on our Savior and living a life for His glory, not glory from the world. We no longer need to worry about what the world thinks because what we see and how we present ourselves has been "renewed . . . according to the image of [our] Creator" (Colossians 3:10 CSB). What a blessing!

Colossians 3:1–10 (CSB)

ETERNAL OVER EARTHLY

So if you have been raised with Christ, seek the things above, where Christ is, seated at the right hand of God. Set your minds on things above, not on earthly things. For you died, and your life is hidden with Christ in God. When Christ, who is your life, appears, then you also will appear with Him in glory. Therefore, put to death what belongs to your earthly nature: sexual immorality, impurity, lust, evil desire, and greed, which is idolatry. Because of these, God's wrath is coming upon the disobedient, and you once walked in these things when you were living in them. But now, put away all the following: anger, wrath, malice, slander, and filthy language from your mouth. Do not lie to one another, since you have put off the old self with its practices and have put on the new self. You are being renewed in knowledge according to the image of your Creator.

Reflect

Who is the author of this passage? Who is the audience?

How do you think this passage impacted the audience?

Reflect

What do you see about the Lord?

What key themes do you see?

Verse Breakdown

- given a new life (eternal life) as a result of accepting Christ as Lord & Savior.

"So if you have been **raised with Christ**, seek the things above, where Christ is, seated at the right hand of God. Set your minds on things above, not on earthly things."

Colossians 3:1-2
CSB

- a position of power.

- He is seated because His work is finished. He does not have to stand ready because He already has victory over death!

- "Things above" ↳ eternal things, things that matter to God. ↳ see vv. 12-15

- anger, malice, immorality, etc. (vv 8-9). ↳ many of these things have been deemed acceptable by culture, but they are not of God.

- Eternal over earthly, always.

In light of what you learned and observed, how can you apply this to your life and/or how should you respond to the Lord?

_____
_____
_____
_____
_____

Other Scriptures to consider
I JOHN 2:15-17 | MATTHEW 6:19-21

DAY 4

So don't be afraid; you are worth
more than many sparrows.

MATTHEW 10:31 CSB

He Knows Us and Sees Us

When you start studying today's passage, you may be confused. You may think: Um, Carrie? What is this? This passage doesn't start out well. You're right. It doesn't, but hang in there with me, and we'll get to the beautiful promise at the end.

Life is really good at kicking us while we're down. Sometimes it feels like one thing after another. Other times, things are going well, and then out of nowhere, we're hit with a circumstance that shakes everything. On some level, everyone who went through 2020 felt this. We went from life being normal to life being completely upside down. Maybe you had to suddenly homeschool your kids. Maybe you lost your job. Maybe you lost a friend or family member. In any hard circumstance, it's tempting to wonder if God is there. It's easy to feel as if He just checked out and forgot about you.

Friend, please don't believe this.

In this passage, Jesus had just commissioned the disciples. He told them what their job was and what would happen as a result. We often think the disciples had it pretty easy since they had God in human form on their side and all, but the reality is the opposite. They had very few supplies, and they traveled from town to town not knowing how they would eat or where they would sleep. When they arrived at those places, they weren't always welcomed. They were hated for the message of the Messiah they shared. If it were me in their place, I would wonder where God is. God, You literally told me to go here. Why am I being treated so poorly? Are You even here? Did You forget about me?

Jesus reminded the disciples—and He reminds us—that God has not forgotten us. Not only does He not forget, but He is hyperaware of us. In fact, He knows every little detail of our lives.

I love the comparison of the sparrows. At the time, sparrows were bought and sold and were similar to the birds used for sacrifice at the temple. In Leviticus 5, the Lord tells Moses all the animals that can be used for sacrifice. Birds are toward the end of the list as acceptable sacrifices for the poorest people. It's clear that these birds held little value, but Jesus said God pays attention to every one of them! If He sees every sparrow, how much more does He see you—His child created in His image? He absolutely sees what happens in your life.

This can be hard to accept when we're going through difficulties, but don't ever forget that God loves you, He knows you, and He sees you.

Verse Breakdown

- Half a penny per sparrow.
  ↓
  obvious, but really points out how little people valued them

- small bird that over populated the area - they were in plentiful supply so they were sold as food for those who were poor.

> "Are not two **sparrows** sold for a penny? Yet not one of them will fall to the ground outside your **Father's** care."
>
> **Matthew 10:29**
> NIV

- intentional choice of language. A father cares for his children in a personal way.

- Not a single sparrow is forgotten or unknown by God.

- If the Lord cares for the "insignificant" in this way, imagine the care and love He has for us - the only creation He made in His own image.

- V. 31 "You are worth more than many sparrows."

Your turn! Turn the page and use the margins provided to break down Scripture for yourself.

Once you've completed the "Reflect" section, come back and make a note of how you can apply this Scripture to your life and/or how you should respond to the Lord in light of what you've observed.

_____
_____
_____
_____
_____
_____

Matthew 10:22-31 (CSB)

HE KNOWS US AND SEES US

"You will be hated by everyone because of My name. But the one who endures to the end will be saved. When they persecute you in one town, flee to another. For truly I tell you, you will not have gone through the towns of Israel before the Son of Man comes. A disciple is not above his teacher, or a slave above his master. It is enough for a disciple to become like his teacher and a slave like his master. If they called the head of the house 'Beelzebul,' how much more the members of his household!

"Therefore, don't be afraid of them, since there is nothing covered that won't be uncovered and nothing hidden that won't be made known. What I tell you in the dark, speak in the light. What you hear in a whisper, proclaim on the housetops. Don't fear those who kill the body but are not able to kill the soul; rather, fear him who is able to destroy both soul and body in hell. Aren't two sparrows sold for a penny? Yet not one of them falls to the ground without your Father's consent. But even the hairs of your head have all been counted. So don't be afraid; you are worth more than many sparrows."

Other Scriptures to consider
LUKE 12:22-31 | PSALM 145:14-21 | LUKE 6:22-23

Reflect

Who is the author of this passage? Who is the audience?

How do you think this passage impacted the audience?

Reflect

What do you see about the Lord?

What key themes do you see?

DAY 5

Therefore, as God's chosen ones, holy and dearly loved, put on compassion, kindness, humility, gentleness, and patience, bearing with one another and forgiving one another if anyone has a grievance against another

COLOSSIANS 3:12–13 CSB

Called and Chosen, and Our Response

I'm going to tell on myself here. My default emotion when things are hard is anger. It's something I'm constantly working on and something the Lord convicts me of often. Most of the time, the root of my anger and stress is my need for control. I like to have a plan. If you ask me to go somewhere but don't tell me where to park, I'm probably not coming. I struggle with severe anxiety, and my anxiety presents as anger in most situations. While it's frustrating to feel this way, it's also a blessing because my anger is a reminder of how I can better reflect Jesus.

This passage starts with the word "therefore," which usually tells us to look back at what we just read so we can keep it in mind for the next part. In this case, Paul told the church at Colossae what to turn away from. He doesn't leave them hanging though. He goes on to tell them how they should act: They should forgive, love, and be kind. And they should be patient and humble. These are wonderful things to emulate in our lives. You may even recognize some as fruit of the Spirit, but why we do these things is what matters most.

When I'm angry, I feel it, and I try to take a step back and ask myself, "Is this posture glorifying to God?" It's hard to be patient with tiny humans who don't listen to you. It's hard to be kind to someone who walks all over you at work; it's hard to forgive someone who has wronged you—but Christ does all those things for us! Because we are chosen by God (which is incredible), loved by Him, and forgiven by Him, we ought to love and forgive others.

One last thing that sticks out to me in this passage is the verse about the peace of Christ. Peace isn't just something Christ gives—it's something God *is*. In the book of Judges, Gideon meets the angel of the Lord and later builds an altar, calling it Yahweh Shalom, or "The Lord Is Peace" (6:24). When we allow the peace of the Lord to fill our hearts, we're allowing *Him* to fill our hearts. This means we are not only able to experience the peace He brings, but we're also able to receive the love, kindness, forgiveness, and humility required to reflect Christ as Paul encourages the Colossians to do.

Maybe you also struggle with anger, or maybe there's something else that gets in your way. I encourage you to use this passage as a motivator and reminder. Let everything we do, whether in word or deed, reflect Christ and bring Him glory. Are we going to do this perfectly? Of course not! But let's try!

Colossians 3:12-17 (CSB)

CALLED AND CHOSEN, AND OUR RESPONSE

Therefore, as God's chosen ones, holy and dearly loved, put on compassion, kindness, humility, gentleness, and patience, bearing with one another and forgiving one another if anyone has a grievance against another. Just as the Lord has forgiven you, so you are also to forgive. Above all, put on love, which is the perfect bond of unity. And let the peace of Christ, to which you were also called in one body, rule your hearts. And be thankful. Let the word of Christ dwell richly among you, in all wisdom teaching and admonishing one another through psalms, hymns, and spiritual songs, singing to God with gratitude in your hearts. And whatever you do, in word or in deed, do everything in the name of the Lord Jesus, giving thanks to God the Father through Him.

Reflect

Who is the author of this passage? Who is the audience?

How do you think this passage impacted the audience?

Reflect

What do you see about the Lord?

What key themes do you see?

Verse Breakdown

Annotations around the verse:

- **Scripture**
- **dwell** — to be within, to live, to take residence in
- *a reminder to not let scripture go in one ear & out the other.*
- The Word is encouraging, but that's not all it is! In order to be more like Christ, let the word teach & refine us as it also encourages us.
- Not out of obligation, but recognizing the gift God has given us in His Word
- Always, in all ways. Do everything for His glory!

> "Let the word of Christ (dwell) richly among you, in all wisdom teaching and admonishing one another through psalms, hymns, and spiritual songs, singing to God with gratitude in your hearts. And whatever you do, in word or in deed, do everything in the name of the Lord Jesus, giving thanks to God the Father through him."

Colossians 3:16-17
CSB

Thank you, Lord, for the gift of Your Word!

In light of what you learned and observed, how can you apply this to your life and/or how should you respond to the Lord?

_____
_____
_____
_____
_____
_____

Other Scriptures to consider

I CORINTHIANS 13:1-7 | I JOHN 4:7-21 | GALATIANS 3:23-29

DAY 6

He is like a tree planted beside flowing streams that bears its fruit in its season, and its leaf does not wither.

PSALM 1:3 CSB

Joy Is Found in the Lord

I love this psalm. I love it because it reminds me where my joy is. When I really started studying the Bible, I fell in love with it. I was drawn to the story, the teaching, and the encouragement, but I was deeply drawn to the joy I felt as I read it. Being in the Word of God brings me so much comfort, and that's exactly what this psalm says it does.

When I read Psalm 1, I'm reminded of the parable of the sower in Matthew 13. In this parable, Jesus taught about seeds (the Word of God) that were sown in different kinds of soil, and He described what each soil type represented. Some seeds fell on rocky ground; others fell into thorns. These seeds failed to thrive. But the seeds that fell on the good soil grew strong and were fruitful. That good soil represents a heart that is open to understanding Scripture. When we know and understand Scripture, we give ourselves roots that are deep and nourished. Our roots are strong when we're rooted in the Word of God. When Christ is our foundation, we can be delighted in His Word because we know it's truth. We know Jesus has the ultimate victory, we know He is the One who sustains us, and we know joy is found in Him, because His Word says so!

Psalm 1:1–6 (CSB)

JOY IS FOUND IN THE LORD

How happy is the one who does not walk in the advice of the wicked or stand in the pathway with sinners or sit in the company of mockers! Instead, his delight is in the Lord's instruction, and he meditates on it day and night. He is like a tree planted beside flowing streams that bears its fruit in its season, and its leaf does not wither. Whatever he does prospers. The wicked are not like this; instead, they are like chaff that the wind blows away. Therefore the wicked will not stand up in the judgment, nor sinners in the assembly of the righteous. For the Lord watches over the way of the righteous, but the way of the wicked leads to ruin.

Reflect

Who is the author of this passage? Who is the audience?

How do you think this passage impacted the audience?

Reflect

What do you see about the Lord?

_____
_____
_____
_____
_____
_____
_____
_____
_____
_____
_____

What key themes do you see?

_____
_____
_____
_____
_____
_____
_____
_____
_____
_____
_____

Verse Breakdown

- Instead of what?
V.1 - instead of walking in the way of the wicked or pursuing a life of sin.

"Instead, his delight is in the Lord's instruction, and he meditates on it day and night."

Psalm 1:2
CSB

- The Word of God.

- Not just in hard seasons. Not when we need something. Not when it's convenient. The Word of God should be a part of our lives every moment of every day.

- Hebrew word "haga" - to moan, growl, utter, muse, mutter, meditate, devise, plot, seek.

- These are not abstract verbs - they reflect action

- Meditation on the Word is not a passive thing!

In light of what you learned and observed, how can you apply this to your life and/or how should you respond to the Lord?

_____
_____
_____
_____
_____

Other Scriptures to consider
MATTHEW 13:1-9 | PSALM 119:9-16 | MATTHEW 7:13-14

DAY 7

Because He is at my right hand,
I will not be shaken.

PSALM 16:8 CSB

In His Presence Is Abundance of Joy

When I was seven months pregnant, our house flooded. We had to move out of our home with no time frame of when our house would be safe to live in. Shortly after, I was admitted to the hospital and gave birth to my daughter six weeks early. When she was taken to the Neonatal Intensive Care Unit, or NICU, minutes after she was born, I felt completely lost. I had no home, my baby was sick, and I had no idea what was going to happen. I missed out on baby showers and leaving the hospital with my daughter. I thought for sure I would also miss out on bringing her to her real home since we were still displaced. Nevertheless, I was confident that God knew what He was doing, and that's the only thing that kept me feeling peace in the storm.

Your Bible may have a header that says "A Miktam of David" above this psalm. This usually means the psalm was written during a time of trouble. David was in trouble, and the Lord was the only good thing in his life. He was unsure about nearly everything, but he knew that God was good, and this knowledge allowed him to rest during the struggle.

We can learn from David. We can be content in all circumstances because we know God is good. Looking back at my daughter's birth, God had us in His hands the whole time. While her NICU stay was incredibly difficult, I remembered that God is sovereign and His timing is perfect. A few days after I was discharged, our house was finished, and two weeks later, we were able to bring our baby home.

God holds our future, and I don't know about you, but if my life is in anyone's hands, I'm glad it's His! I'm glad the One who holds me is the One who is sovereign over everything.

Verse Breakdown

- **Two fold meaning:**
  - praise in the dark times of life.
  - praise at all hours, never ceasing.

- He is the Wonderful counselor! (Is. 9:6)

- Davids heart was dedicated to the Word of God. We can't follow our emotions but we can (and should) follow the Word of God. & our hearts should be focused on Him.

> "I will praise the Lord, who counsels me; even at night my heart instructs me. I keep my eyes always on the Lord. With him at my right hand, I will not be shaken."
>
> **Psalm 16:7-8**
> NIV

- Our feet follow where our eyes go. If we focus on the things of the world we will follow the world, but if our focus is on God, we will walk towards Him.

- This doesn't say, "I will always have an easy time." It says that, no matter the circumstance, the Lord is a firm foundation.

Your turn! Turn the page and use the margins provided to break down Scripture for yourself.

Once you've completed the "Reflect" section, come back and make a note of how you can apply this Scripture to your life and/or how you should respond to the Lord in light of what you've observed.

_____
_____
_____
_____
_____
_____

Psalm 16:1–11 (CSB)

IN HIS PRESENCE IS
ABUNDANCE OF JOY

A Miktam of David.

Protect me, God, for I take refuge in You. I said to the LORD, "You are my Lord; I have nothing good besides You." As for the holy people who are in the land, they are the noble ones. All my delight is in them. The sorrows of those who take another god for themselves will multiply; I will not pour out their drink offerings of blood, and I will not speak their names with my lips. LORD, You are my portion and my cup of blessing; You hold my future. The boundary lines have fallen for me in pleasant places; indeed, I have a beautiful inheritance. I will bless the LORD who counsels me—even at night when my thoughts trouble me. I always let the LORD guide me. Because He is at my right hand, I will not be shaken. Therefore my heart is glad and my whole being rejoices; my body also rests securely. For You will not abandon me to Sheol; You will not allow Your faithful one to see decay. You reveal the path of life to me; in Your presence is abundant joy; at Your right hand are eternal pleasures.

Other Scriptures to consider
PSALM 62:1-8 | MATTHEW 8:23-27 | PHILIPPIANS 4:6-7

Reflect

Who is the author of this passage? Who is the audience?

How do you think this passage impacted the audience?

Reflect

What do you see about the Lord?

What key themes do you see?

DAY 8

**For you are saved by grace through faith,
and this is not from yourselves; it is God's gift.**

EPHESIANS 2:8 CSB

The Beauty of the Gospel

Many of us know the story of Adam and Eve well. God gave them everything they needed, and the only thing they were not supposed to do was eat from the tree of the knowledge of good and evil (Genesis 2:17). What did they do? They ate from the tree of the knowledge of good and evil. We know the story, but do we really understand the importance of it? That act of disobedience set a precedent for all of us.

The consequence for sin is death; this is clear throughout the Bible (Romans 6:23). Because of Adam and Eve, we all start from that sinful place. I know this doesn't sound very encouraging, but look at Ephesians 2:4–5. We were dead in our sins, *"but God . . . made us alive with Christ"* (emphasis added).

I love seeing the *"but God"* moments in the Bible. They're an amazing reminder of what God can do in any situation. Adam and Eve sinned, but God spared their lives. The people of Israel escaped slavery only to be chased and trapped at the Red Sea, but God split the sea, securing their freedom. We sin regularly, which separates us from God, but God sent Jesus to bear the consequence of our sin so we would no longer be separated from Him.

Even better, we don't have to do anything to receive this grace, which can be hard to rationalize. The world we live in operates based on exchanges and trades. Sometimes this is obvious, maybe exchanging money for goods and services or trading time with someone. Other times, it's less obvious. For example, we do something for a neighbor and expect them to help us in return at some point. If this is our mindset when interacting with people, it's hard to understand how God could forgive us without our having to do anything for that forgiveness. But, friends, that's the reality and beauty of the gospel, and that's what Paul tells the Ephesus church in this passage.

We are saved by grace through faith. There is nothing we can do on our own to gain salvation. The only thing we need to do is have faith that Christ died in our place. What a gift!

Ephesians 2:1-10 (CSB)

THE BEAUTY OF THE GOSPEL

You were dead in your trespasses and sins in which you previously walked according to the ways of this world, according to the ruler of the power of the air, the spirit now working in the disobedient. We too all previously lived among them in our fleshly desires, carrying out the inclinations of our flesh and thoughts, and we were by nature children under wrath as the others were also. But God, who is rich in mercy, because of His great love that He had for us, made us alive with Christ even though we were dead in trespasses. You are saved by grace! He also raised us up with

Him and seated us with Him in the heavens in Christ Jesus, so that in the coming ages He might display the immeasurable riches of His grace through His kindness to us in Christ Jesus. For you are saved by grace through faith, and this is not from yourselves; it is God's gift—not from works, so that no one can boast. For we are His workmanship, created in Christ Jesus for good works, which God prepared ahead of time for us to do.

Reflect

Who is the author of this passage? Who is the audience?

How do you think this passage impacted the audience?

Reflect

What do you see about the Lord?

What key themes do you see?

Verse Breakdown

- This verse shares something that is in contrast to the prior verse.
- Mercy is not in limited or short supply.
- Salvation is because of God's grace, not because of anything we do!

"But God, who is rich in mercy, because of his great love that he had for us, made us alive with Christ even though we were dead in trespasses. You are saved by grace!"

Ephesians 2:4-5
CSB

- God loved us while we were still sinners — we should have been dead to Him, but He extended His love to us anyway.
- Not by works! Grace is a gift! ↳ Eph. 2:8-9

In light of what you learned and observed, how can you apply this to your life and/or how should you respond to the Lord?

_____
_____
_____
_____
_____

Other Scriptures to consider
JOHN 3:15-17 | MICAH 7:18-20 | TITUS 3:4-7 | ROMANS 6:4-11

DAY 9

Now to Him who is able to do immeasurably more than all we ask or imagine, according to His power that is at work within us, to Him be glory in the church and in Christ Jesus throughout all generations, for ever and ever! Amen.

EPHESIANS 3:20–21 NIV

More Than We Can Ask or Imagine

When I was a kid, my parents listened to a lot of acapella music. I remember many car rides in our Mercury Villager minivan as we listened to cassette tapes of different acapella groups singing about the Lord. One of the songs we listened to often was directly from this passage: "Now to Him who is able to do immeasurably more than all we ask or imagine . . ." (verse 20).

Even as a child, this verse stuck out to me. God is able to do immeasurably more than all we could ever ask or imagine. Even now, the more I think about it, the bigger my God becomes. I don't know about you, but I could ask for a lot of things, and my imagination isn't in short supply. Scripture tells us that God can do immeasurably more than that! There is no ceiling—no limit—on what the Lord can do in our lives.

So why do we sometimes think our burdens are too much for Him?

Life can be challenging. We can feel overwhelmed by circumstances, hurt by those we care about, and angry with ourselves. There have been times in my life where it seemed like everything that could go wrong was going wrong. I've felt lost, hurt, and abandoned. Life can feel out of control sometimes, and it's in our nature to feel that if we can't control something, then no one can. May I encourage you, though? Even when we feel as if no one can control what we're going through, we have a God who can and does control it all.

Not only can He understand our situations, He can also work through them in ways we can't even imagine. This gives me so much hope, and I hope it does the same for you!

Verse Breakdown

"Now to him who is able to do above and beyond all that we ask or think according to the power that works in us to him be glory in the church and in Christ Jesus to all generations, forever and ever. Amen."

Ephesians 3:20-21
CSB

- He is able
- "immeasurably more" → We have limited ability. God is able to do more than we can even imagine!
- A big reason why we should trust His timing & His sovereignty. He has the full picture, far beyond our understanding!
- Not Paul or any other apostle or teacher who came to share the gospel. To HIM be the glory!
- The same power that can do immeasurably more is the power that works within us.
  - This does NOT mean we have power like God. It means God's power is at work within us.
- The gospel is for everyone, Jesus deserves eternal glory throughout all generations.

Your turn! Turn the page and use the margins provided to break down Scripture for yourself.

Once you've completed the "Reflect" section, come back and make a note of how you can apply this Scripture to your life and/or how you should respond to the Lord in light of what you've observed.

Ephesians 3:14-21 (NIV)

MORE THAN WE CAN ASK OR IMAGINE

For this reason I kneel before the Father, from whom every family in heaven and on earth derives its name. I pray that out of His glorious riches He may strengthen you with power through His Spirit in your inner being, so that Christ may dwell in your hearts through faith. And I pray that you, being rooted and established in love, may have power, together with all the Lord's holy people, to grasp how wide and long and high and deep is the love of Christ, and to know this love that surpasses knowledge—that you may be filled to the measure of all the fullness of God.

Now to Him who is able to do immeasurably more than all we ask or imagine, according to His power that is at work within us, to Him be glory in the church and in Christ Jesus throughout all generations, for ever and ever! Amen.

Other Scriptures to consider
*JEREMIAH 32:17–27 | DANIEL 3
PSALM 29 | EPHESIANS 1:18–23*

Reflect

Who is the author of this passage? Who is the audience?

How do you think this passage impacted the audience?

Reflect

What do you see about the Lord?

What key themes do you see?

DAY 10

Be strengthened by the Lord and by His vast strength.

EPHESIANS 6:10 CSB

Our Spiritual Armor

The passage we're digging into today gets me fired up. Symbolism is prevalent in the Bible, but the layers of meaning in today's passage in particular make this passage just come alive. Paul closes his letter to the church in Ephesus by instructing them to prepare themselves as if they're going into battle. Soldiers needed many things to make sure they could fight properly. They needed a belt, traditionally used in battle to keep garments under armor secure and out of the way. Armor on the chest protected vital organs; good shoes were crucial in battle as terrain was unpredictable; a shield was needed to block attacks; helmets protected the head from lethal blows; and a sword was necessary to use as a weapon and defense.

So why does this excite me? Because this passage tells us exactly what we need to stand firm in our faith, and it tells us how to use these things. Truth, like a belt, is first. Without a foundation in biblical truth, our fight is useless, much like a soldier's fight was useless if he failed to wear a belt to gather up his garments. It was impossible to fight efficiently without good shoes, and it's impossible for us to respond to circumstances well without understanding the gospel and the peace that comes with it. The shield of faith is our protection from the lies of the enemy, and the knowledge and hope we have from our salvation protect our minds like a helmet.

Just because a soldier owned these pieces of armor meant nothing unless he put them on. That's why Paul says to put on the full armor of God—not just a few pieces of it. We can't put on faith and hope and truth but fail to remember the Word of God—our sword—and expect to fight our battles well. It's important to make sure we're completely ready! Thankfully, this armor isn't a secret, and it isn't hidden. Since we have access to all these things, let's intentionally choose to utilize them on a daily basis.

How can we do this? It starts by getting into the Word of God and spending time with Him daily. If you're reading this, you're off to a great start!

Ephesians 6:10-18 (CSB)

THE BEAUTY OF THE GOSPEL

Finally, be strengthened by the Lord and by His vast strength. Put on the full armor of God so that you can stand against the schemes of the devil. For our struggle is not against flesh and blood, but against the rulers, against the authorities, against the cosmic powers of this darkness, against evil, spiritual forces in the heavens. For this reason take up the full armor of God, so that you may be able to resist in the evil day, and having prepared everything, to take your stand. Stand, therefore, with truth like a belt around your waist, righteousness like armor on your chest, and your feet sandaled with readiness for the gospel of peace. In every situation take up the shield of faith with which you can extinguish all the flaming arrows of the evil one. Take the helmet of salvation and the sword of the Spirit—which is the word of God. Pray at all times in the Spirit with every prayer and request, and stay alert with all perseverance and intercession for all the saints.

Reflect

Who is the author of this passage? Who is the audience?

How do you think this passage impacted the audience?

Reflect

What do you see about the Lord?

_____
_____
_____
_____
_____
_____
_____
_____
_____
_____
_____
_____

What key themes do you see?

_____
_____
_____
_____
_____
_____
_____
_____
_____
_____
_____
_____

Verse Breakdown

We can't just partially prepare for battle!

● Be equipped with the full armor of God → Truth, Righteousness, Peace, Faith, Salvation, The Word of God.

"Put on the full armor of God so that you can stand against the schemes of the devil."

Ephesians 6:11
CSB

● The enemy doesn't trick us accidentally. He knows our doubts & our weaknesses & uses them to pull us away from God. It is intentional!

● Without the armor of God, we aren't ready to stand against the enemy. Saying "No" to sin is HARD. We are far less likely to fall into his traps when we are covered in His armor.

In light of what you learned and observed, how can you apply this to your life and/or how should you respond to the Lord?

___
___
___
___
___

Other Scriptures to consider
II CORINTHIANS 10:3–5 | I THESSALONIANS 5:8
ROMANS 12:11–12 | I PETER 5:8–9

DAY 11

O LORD, you have searched me and known me!

PSALM 139:1 ESV

Hemmed In, Behind and Before

Today, we are going to dive into a verse that is such an encouragement to me. When I was younger, I suffered from an eating disorder that nearly killed me. As much as I would love to say I am completely recovered, I'm not. While I'm not engaging in eating disorder behaviors, I still very much struggle with how I look. I'm thankful that these thoughts aren't as common as they used to be, but right now I'm struggling. In times like these, I'm especially thankful for the Word of God.

This verse isn't just about body image, but it can be a helpful Scripture to remember when we feel self-conscious because it reminds us we are "fearfully and wonderfully made." I find even more comfort, however, in verse 5: "You hem me in, behind and before, and lay your hand upon me."

I like the ESV translation of this because of the imagery it gives. When we hem a garment, we're finishing it. We're surrounding fabric with stitching so the garment remains intact and doesn't fray. When you hem something, you gather up its rough edges and create a clean edge that prolongs the life of the garment and keeps it from falling apart over time. This is what God does for us. In the times when we feel frayed and falling apart, God hems us in. He comes in behind us and before us and puts His hands on our frayed edges.

This is so encouraging! In the midst of our struggles and hard times, we can rest knowing that God sees it all, knows it all, and is there behind and before it. We aren't hidden from Him, and we never have been. When I'm feeling insecure, I know that God is there with me. I don't understand why I struggle so much with this particular thing. I've been angry about it. It's felt unfair. But ultimately, I find rest knowing that God is fighting this battle for me, and He hears me when I'm struggling. Nothing I go through is for no reason. God is behind, before, and within it all.

Verse Breakdown

- omnipresence & sovereignty of God.

"Where can I go from your Spirit? Where can I flee from your presence? If I go up to the heavens, you are there; if I make my bed in the depths, you are there. If I rise on the wings of the dawn, if I settle on the far side of the sea, even there your hand will guide me, your right hand will hold me fast."

Psalm 139:7-10
NIV

- He guides us, even when we try to flee.
    ↓
- reminds us of the grace of God.

- even in the darkest, most confusing, distant places, the Lord is there.

- Not a loose grip - He holds us firmly!

Nothing can separate us from the love of God! (Rom. 8:38-39)

Your turn! Turn the page and use the margins provided to break down Scripture for yourself.

Once you've completed the "Reflect" section, come back and make a note of how you can apply this Scripture to your life and/or how you should respond to the Lord in light of what you've observed.

_____
_____
_____
_____

Other Scriptures to consider
GENESIS 1:17-26 | ISAIAH 55:6-9 | HEBREWS 4:13-16

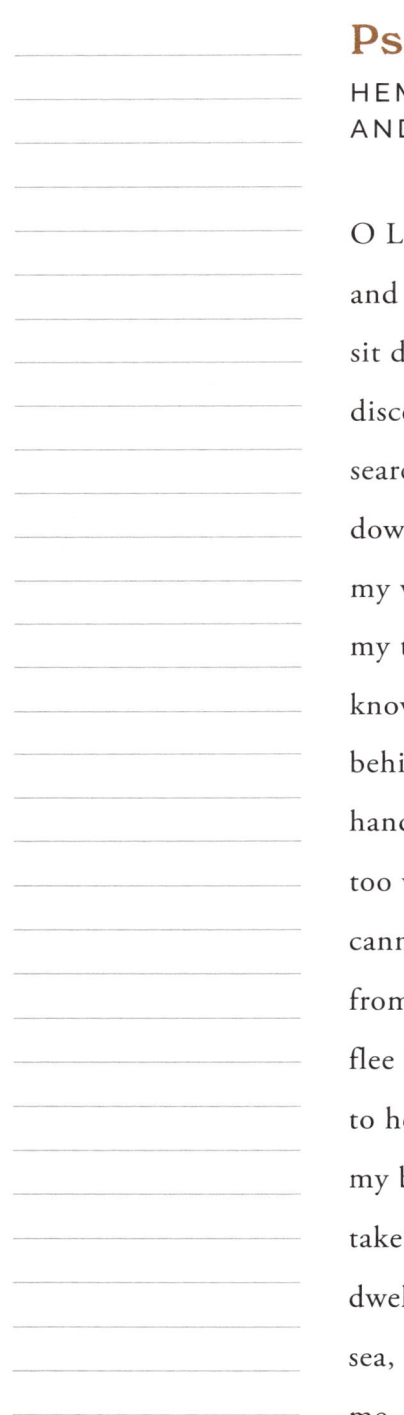

Psalm 139:1–18 (ESV)

HEMMED IN, BEHIND AND BEFORE

O Lord, you have searched me and known me! You know when I sit down and when I rise up; you discern my thoughts from afar. You search out my path and my lying down and are acquainted with all my ways. Even before a word is on my tongue, behold, O Lord, you know it altogether. You hem me in, behind and before, and lay your hand upon me. Such knowledge is too wonderful for me; it is high; I cannot attain it. Where shall I go from your Spirit? Or where shall I flee from your presence? If I ascend to heaven, you are there! If I make my bed in Sheol, you are there! If I take the wings of the morning and dwell in the uttermost parts of the sea, even there your hand shall lead me, and your right hand shall hold me. If I say, "Surely the darkness shall cover me, and the light about me be night," even the darkness is not dark to you; the night is bright as the day, for darkness is as light with you. For you formed my inward parts; you knitted me together in my mother's womb. I praise you, for I am fearfully and wonderfully made. Wonderful are your works; my soul knows it very well. My frame was not hidden from you, when I was being made in secret, intricately woven in the depths of the earth. Your eyes saw my unformed substance; in your book were written, every one of them, the days that were formed for me, when as yet there was none of them. How precious to me are your thoughts, O God! How vast is the sum of them! If I would count them, they are more than the sand. I awake, and I am still with you.

Reflect

Who is the author of this passage? Who is the audience?

How do you think this passage impacted the audience?

Reflect

What do you see about the Lord?

What key themes do you see?

DAY 12

God shows his love for us in that while we were still sinners, Christ died for us.

ROMANS 5:8 ESV

All Access through Jesus

Many Christians learn the verse Romans 5:8 early on. It's the gospel in a nutshell, as many passages written by Paul are. Verse 8 on its own is wonderful, but reading it in context makes it even more powerful. In this passage, Paul reminds us that the grace of God is a gift. John writes that we have received "grace upon grace" (John 1:16 ESV), but Paul uses the word "access" in Romans 5:2 to describe the way we receive that gift. This may seem small, but it's one of my biggest takeaways from this passage.

Before Christ died on the cross, only the high priests could enter the holy of holies and be in the Lord's presence, and they could only do this once a year. The idea that any person could be in the presence of God was unheard of and, in the Old Testament, warranted death. For Paul to tell the church that they had direct access to God themselves would have been a huge shift. This change in mindset showed the goodness and love of God in a way they could understand.

God gives us access to Himself and His grace even though we don't deserve it. Verse 8 reminds us that Christ died for us "while we were still sinners." We couldn't do anything to make ourselves "good enough" and convince Him to die on a cross for us. He did it because He loves us and wanted to give us access to His grace so we could have an intimate relationship with our heavenly Father. What a testament to the power of the blood of Jesus!

Romans 5:1–11 (ESV)
ALL ACCESS THROUGH JESUS

Therefore, since we have been justified by faith, we have peace with God through our Lord Jesus Christ. Through him we have also obtained access by faith into this grace in which we stand, and we rejoice in hope of the glory of God. Not only that, but we rejoice in our sufferings, knowing that suffering produces endurance, and endurance produces character, and character produces hope, and hope does not put us to shame, because God's love has been poured into our hearts through the Holy Spirit who has been given to us. For while we were still weak, at the right time Christ died for the ungodly. For one will scarcely die for a righteous person—though perhaps for a good person one would dare even to die—but God shows his love for us in that while we were still sinners, Christ died for us. Since, therefore, we have now been justified by his blood, much more shall we be saved by him from the wrath of God. For if while we were enemies we were reconciled to God by the death of his Son, much more, now that we are reconciled, shall we be saved by his life. More than that, we also rejoice in God through our Lord Jesus Christ, through whom we have now received reconciliation.

Reflect

Who is the author of this passage? Who is the audience?

How do you think this passage impacted the audience?

Reflect

What do you see about the Lord?

What key themes do you see?

Verse Breakdown

- calls reader to the previous verse for context.

This verse notes a contrast to the ideas in vv. 6-7

"demonstrates" - to show, establish, exhibit.

The love of God himself to us - this is a big deal! God himself loves each of us and knows us, specifically.

"But God proves his own love for us in that while we were still sinners, Christ died for us."

Romans 5:8
CSB

Jesus didn't die for us when we were good (we aren't righteous), Jesus died for us while we were still sinners.

↳ The ultimate example of Matt. 5:43-48

The perfect sacrifice.

→ His sacrifice is profound because it is proof of God's love for us. He sent His son to die for us, to save us from eternal separation from Him, even though we did not deserve it.

In light of what you learned and observed, how can you apply this to your life and/or how should you respond to the Lord?

_____
_____
_____
_____
_____
_____

Other Scriptures to consider
EPHESIANS 2:11-20 | EPHESIANS 3:6-13 | HEBREWS 10:19-25 | JOHN 1:14-18

DAY 13

If God is for us, who is against us?

ROMANS 8:31 CSB

Never Forgotten

In my family, the past ten years have been a struggle. For a long time, one of my family members seemed to have forgotten about us. Our calls weren't returned, birthday cards stopped coming, and after a while, we all assumed this person just didn't love us anymore. It was heartbreaking. We weren't sure what happened or why the distance seemed to grow over the years; it was hard to accept that they had forgotten about us.

I'm grateful these broken relationships have started the restoration process, but I wonder how many of us feel like this has happened between us and God. Maybe we've been distant from Him, or maybe we think too much in our lives has gone wrong and He's forgotten about us. But remember, God isn't a family member—He's the Lord of creation. People abandon us, but God never will. When Paul wrote to Rome, he told the people exactly that. Nothing can separate us from the love of God.

As I thought about this passage in my quiet time one morning, I made a connection I hadn't made before. I've had Romans 8:38–39 memorized since I was a child, but reading it in the context of what Christ did for me brought a whole new revelation. God gave us Jesus, His Son, knowing that Jesus would be sacrificed for our sins. This seems like an abstract concept, but think about it literally. If God, a father, knew a specific sin or circumstance could separate us from His love, would He have sacrificed His son? I don't know about you, but I don't think God would send His only Son as a sacrifice if He knew we could lose His love.

This truth is such good news! Not only is it a comfort when we feel like we're far from Him, but it also reminds us that God's love is relentless. And because He has victory over death, we have nothing to fear. The One who sacrificed Himself for us sits in power at the right hand of the Father. He doesn't resent us for our sin but advocates for us when we put our faith in Him!

Verse Breakdown

Paul covers both the seen & unseen
↳ *angels nor rulers (demons, in other translations) & height or death.*

Paul, writing to the Roman church

"For I am persuaded that neither death nor life, nor angels nor rulers, nor things present nor things to come, nor powers, nor height nor depth, nor any other created thing will be able to separate us from the love of God that is in Christ Jesus our Lord."

Romans 8:38-39
CSB

A blanket statement in recognition of our lack of understanding
↳ *prompts us to humility*

His love for us is evident by the work Jesus did on the cross.
↳ *prompts us to worship*

Nothing can separate us from the love of God.

Your turn! Turn the page and use the margins provided to break down Scripture for yourself.

Once you've completed the "Reflect" section, come back and make a note of how you can apply this Scripture to your life and/or how you should respond to the Lord in light of what you've observed.

Romans 8:31-39 (CSB)

NEVER FORGOTTEN

What, then, are we to say about these things? If God is for us, who is against us? He did not even spare His own Son but gave Him up for us all. How will He not also with Him grant us everything? Who can bring an accusation against God's elect? God is the one who justifies. Who is the one who condemns? Christ Jesus is the one who died, but even more, has been raised; He also is at the right hand of God and intercedes for us. Who can separate us from the love of Christ? Can affliction or distress or persecution or famine or nakedness or danger or sword? As it is written: Because of You we are being put to death all day long; we are counted as sheep to be slaughtered. No, in all these things we are more than conquerors through Him who loved us. For I am persuaded that neither death nor life, nor angels nor rulers, nor things present nor things to come, nor powers, nor height nor depth, nor any other created thing will be able to separate us from the love of God that is in Christ Jesus our Lord.

Other Scriptures to consider
ROMANS 5:8 | EPHESIANS 1:3-8 | I JOHN 4:8-12

Reflect

Who is the author of this passage? Who is the audience?

How do you think this passage impacted the audience?

Reflect

What do you see about the Lord?

What key themes do you see?

DAY 14

Therefore, if anyone is in Christ,
he is a new creation; the old has passed away,
and see, the new has come!

II CORINTHIANS 5:17 CSB

The Old Is Gone; the New Has Come

Have you ever done something you weren't supposed to do and been eaten up with guilt about it? Maybe you said or did something hurtful, and you replayed the situation over and over in your mind wishing you had said or done something different. Or have you ever been in a situation where someone did or said something hurtful to you, and you couldn't let it go? I know I've been on both ends of that situation. Guilt and resentment are hard emotions to navigate. It's even harder when you feel so guilty that you start to think you can never be forgiven.

In II Corinthians, Paul wrote to the church in Corinth. In this passage, he gives comforting words followed by a challenge to those who are in Christ. Here's the comforting part: God knew our sinful nature and loved us anyway; in fact, He loved us so much that He sent Jesus to die on the cross so we could have new life in Him. To God, we are new creations when we come to know Christ. He doesn't hold our past against us. He declares our old self dead because we have been made new through Christ. How amazing is that?

Here's the challenge part: as ambassadors of Christ, we are called to share this good news with others and to see others the same way God sees them. Humanity is sinful and lost and in need of a savior, and we have the amazing opportunity to point them to the One who can make them new.

While we often struggle with giving forgiveness and repairing relationships after being hurt, the Lord doesn't. He's waiting for us to accept His gift of grace. He wants to make us new. If you're in a place where you feel like God can't forgive you, please be comforted knowing that God doesn't hold your past against you. When you come to know Christ and accept Him as your Lord and Savior, your past is erased, and you become a new person. Your debt has been paid. You are forgiven!

II Corinthians 5:16–21 (CSB)

THE OLD IS GONE; THE NEW HAS COME

From now on, then, we do not know anyone from a worldly perspective. Even if we have known Christ from a worldly perspective, yet now we no longer know Him in this way. Therefore, if anyone is in Christ, he is a new creation; the old has passed away, and see, the new has come! Everything is from God, who has reconciled us to Himself through Christ and has given us the ministry of reconciliation. That is, in Christ, God was reconciling the world to Himself, not counting their trespasses against them, and He has committed the message of reconciliation to us. Therefore, we are ambassadors for Christ, since God is making His appeal through us. We plead on Christ's behalf, "Be reconciled to God." He made the one who did not know sin to be sin for us, so that in Him we might become the righteousness of God.

Reflect

Who is the author of this passage? Who is the audience?

How do you think this passage impacted the audience?

Reflect

What do you see about the Lord?

What key themes do you see?

Verse Breakdown

- **What is it there for?** Context! Paul was reminding the church that "we do not know anyone from a world perspective" (v.16) but rather through the lens of the love of God.

- No limits, no disqualifying conditions.

- Not in the world or in tune with "self", but in Christ — a follower of Jesus.

- Completely made new!

- This is a gift! It comes with a responsibility, though. It's our responsibility to walk according to the new life we have in Christ!

> "Therefore, if anyone is in Christ, he is a new creation; the old has passed away, and see, the new has come!"
>
> **2 Corinthians 5:17** CSB

- The old self is dead, does not exist.

- Past sins are not hung over the head of the sinner.

- If the Lord considers our old selves dead, then so should we! → Romans 12:2

In light of what you learned and observed, how can you apply this to your life and/or how should you respond to the Lord?

_____
_____
_____
_____
_____

Other Scriptures to consider
PSALM 51:7-10 | EZEKIEL 36:22-28 | MATTHEW 28:18-20

DAY 15

You meant evil against me, but God meant it for good, to bring it about that many people should be kept alive, as they are today.

GENESIS 50:20 ESV

Meant for Good

When people ask me what my favorite book of the Bible is, I always say Genesis. I love how the entire book sets a perfect foundation for the narrative of the rest of the Bible, and I never get tired of seeing the references to Jesus in the very first book of the Bible. The stories are great, but the idea that God had Jesus in mind from the beginning leaves me in awe.

One of my favorite stories in Genesis is the story of Joseph, and it's my favorite for many reasons. One of them, and maybe the most overlooked reason, is that Israel ended up in Egypt because of Joseph. We often think there's a fault line between Genesis and Exodus, but that isn't the case! Without Joseph ruling over Egypt, there would be no Israel in Egypt and no Israelites for Moses to lead out of Egypt. Moses leading the Israelites out of Egypt is the beginning of Israel's story as a nation, and without Joseph, it wouldn't have happened. Of course, all of this was intricately planned by God, and you may be wondering why I went on a tangent about it. I just get excited about seeing the narrative of the Bible come together.

But, I digress . . .

I won't go over the entire story of Joseph here because it's extensive, and I could probably write a book on that story alone (as you can see from the previous paragraph, I get excited). This passage in particular, however, is such an amazing testament to the Lord and His sovereignty. At this point, Joseph's brothers (the ones who sold him into slavery) are scared that Joseph will kill or enslave them now that their father is dead. What Joseph says to them in Genesis 50:20 is so impactful: "You meant evil against me, but God meant it for good." There's a lot of story that goes with this statement, and I encourage you to read the story of Joseph to get the context, but it's amazing to me on a couple of fronts.

First, Joseph had every right to be angry with his brothers, but he forgives them. Now, would you be jumping at the opportunity to forgive someone who literally sold you into slavery because they were jealous of you? I wouldn't be.

Second, and most importantly, this verse gives us a clear picture of God's plan for us. Many times, we stress about God's plan for our lives. We wonder what His will for us is and why we experience difficult circumstances. This verse is a reminder: no matter what, God can and will use every circumstance for your good and for His glory. Maybe you're in the middle of a storm in your life, and you're exhausted by the wind and the waves that never stop. Friend, I encourage you to rest in the truth of God. Remember that what the enemy intends for evil, God uses for good. It's not always apparent at the moment, but it is biblical truth, and we can trust Him to be faithful!

Verse Breakdown

Quick context - Joseph's brothers sold him into slavery. Joseph ended up second in command over Egypt. Joseph is reunited with his brothers.

● People do evil things. We are sinful by nature.

"You planned evil against me; God planned it for good to bring about the present result—the survival of many people."

Genesis 50:20
CSB

● God is able to redeem any circumstance

● God is sovereign! Joseph didn't have the full picture when he was sold into slavery, but God did and used Joseph to save Israel.

We will go through hard times because we live in a fallen world but we need to remember that our knowledge is limited to our current circumstance. We serve a God who knows it ALL, past, present, and future.

Your turn! Turn the page and use the margins provided to break down Scripture for yourself.

Once you've completed the "Reflect" section, come back and make a note of how you can apply this Scripture to your life and/or how you should respond to the Lord in light of what you've observed.

_____
_____
_____
_____
_____
_____
_____

Genesis 50:15-21 (ESV)

MEANT FOR GOOD

When Joseph's brothers saw that their father was dead, they said, "It may be that Joseph will hate us and pay us back for all the evil that we did to him." So they sent a message to Joseph, saying, "Your father gave this command before he died: 'Say to Joseph, "Please forgive the transgression of your brothers and their sin, because they did evil to you."' And now, please forgive the transgression of the servants of the God of your father." Joseph wept when they spoke to him. His brothers also came and fell down before him and said, "Behold, we are your servants." But Joseph said to them, "Do not fear, for am I in the place of God? As for you, you meant evil against me, but God meant it for good, to bring it about that many people should be kept alive, as they are today. So do not fear; I will provide for you and your little ones." Thus he comforted them and spoke kindly to them.

> **Other Scriptures to consider**
> *GENESIS 45:4-8 | ROMANS 8:28-30 | PSALM 105:16-22*

Reflect

Who is the author of this passage? Who is the audience?

How do you think this passage impacted the audience?

Reflect

What do you see about the Lord?

What key themes do you see?

DAY 16

I will never leave you nor forsake you. Be strong and courageous, because you will lead these people to inherit the land I swore to their ancestors to give them.

JOSHUA 1:5–6 NIV

Being Strong and Courageous

Be strong and courageous. This is such a simple command from the Lord, but it can be so hard to put into practice, right? The command to be strong and courageous is given to Joshua three times in the last four verses of this passage. *Three times.* It seems excessive, but I imagine Joshua was probably feeling a little anxious at this point in his life. His mentor and leader, Moses, had died, and now he was supposed to lead the entire nation of Israel into the promised land. The nation of Israel wasn't just a few thousand people. In Numbers, a census was taken. Only men over the age of twenty were counted in this census, and over 603,550 people were registered! It's safe to assume we can double that number since most men had a wife and one or more children; this means Joshua was leading well over *one million* people into the promised land!

Honestly, I feel anxious just trying to get my husband and daughter through the Nashville Predators crowd at Bridgestone Arena on game night. I can't imagine leading over one million people anywhere!

Here's the thing though: God not only gave Joshua encouragement—He also gave Israel the land. More important than the command to be courageous was God's reminder that He was about to fulfill His promise to Israel. And in a beautiful circle of encouragement, the power that would give Israel the promised land was the power that would protect and be with them wherever they went. God is faithful, and His promises stand. We can be overwhelmed by our circumstances, but in the overwhelming times, we can be encouraged by the unrelenting faithfulness of God.

Joshua 1:1–9 (NIV)

BEING STRONG AND COURAGEOUS

After the death of Moses the servant of the Lord, the Lord said to Joshua son of Nun, Moses' aide: "Moses my servant is dead. Now then, you and all these people, get ready to cross the Jordan River into the land I am about to give to them—to the Israelites. I will give you every place where you set your foot, as I promised Moses. Your territory will extend from the desert to Lebanon, and from the great river, the Euphrates—all the Hittite country—to the Mediterranean Sea in the west. No one will be able to stand against you all the days of your life. As I was with Moses, so I will be with you; I will never leave you nor forsake you. Be strong and courageous, because you will lead these people to inherit the land I swore to their ancestors to give them.

"Be strong and very courageous. Be careful to obey all the law My servant Moses gave you; do not turn from it to the right or to the left, that you may be successful wherever you go. Keep this Book of the Law always on your lips; meditate on it day and night, so that you may be careful to do everything written in it. Then you will be prosperous and successful. Have I not commanded you? Be strong and courageous. Do not be afraid; do not be discouraged, for the Lord your God will be with you wherever you go."

Reflect

Who is the author of this passage? Who is the audience?

How do you think this passage impacted the audience?

Reflect

What do you see about the Lord?

What key themes do you see?

Verse Breakdown

- This wasn't the first time the Lord told Joshua (& the nation of Israel) to be strong & courageous.

- Joshua was on the cusp of entering the Promised Land. Last time he was in this position, Israel rebelled & they were punished to wander. If they did obey this time, they had battles to fight.

- Not a suggestion!

"Haven't I commanded you: be strong and courageous? Do not be afraid or discouraged, for the Lord your God is with you wherever you go."

- The Israelites were God's chosen people!

Joshua 1:9
NIV

- God is omnipresent but also God is sovereign. Not only is the Lord with us, He knows how a situation can be used for good, for His glory.

The Lord went ahead of Israel and they were successful.
↓
His command to not be afraid is a reminder of His peace AND His power.

In light of what you learned and observed, how can you apply this to your life and/or how should you respond to the Lord?

_____
_____
_____
_____

Other Scriptures to consider
DEUTERONOMY 31:1–8 | I CHRONICLES 28 | ISAIAH 41:9–13

DAY 17

He gives strength to the weary and increases the power of the weak. Even youths grow tired and weary, and young men stumble and fall; but those who hope in the Lord will renew their strength. They will soar on wings like eagles; they will run and not grow weary, they will walk and not be faint.

ISAIAH 40:29–31 NIV

Heavenly Strength and Comfort

I will be the first to admit that prophetic books of the Bible really throw me for a loop. The Major Prophets (Isaiah, Jeremiah, Lamentations, Ezekiel, and Daniel) are the primary offenders. They can seem redundant and sad, which makes getting through them difficult. Here's the thing though—they are redundant and sad. These books were written to a broken nation of Israel when they were deep in sin. The broken nation was reminded over and over that they needed to turn from their sin or face complete destruction. What's amazing, though, are the glimpses of hope sprinkled throughout these books that are filled with warnings and calls for repentance.

The Lord speaks through the prophet Isaiah to warn of coming judgment, but He pauses to comfort His people too. He comforts them even though they turned away from Him. The whole book has these moments of comfort, but I love chapter 40. I love how the Lord reminds us that He's in control. He tells us how insignificant people are, comparing us to grasshoppers. I know that doesn't sound very uplifting, but the very next sentence gives us such a beautiful insight into the Lord's love for us. We are like grasshoppers, yet He stretches the heavens over us like a tent to live in. We are small and insignificant compared to the God of creation, yet He cares for us.

The truth of God's provision is all over Scripture, yet we still try to control everything in our lives—things we really have no control over at all—and provide for ourselves. We can all learn from Isaiah's words. The Lord is in control. He created the stars, He knows each of them by name (Psalm 147:4), and He hasn't forgotten a single one. If He knows all that, He surely hasn't forgotten about us. When we grow tired, God doesn't; His strength is infinite. When we lean back and rest in His power, strength, and sovereignty, we're able to experience true rest. Our strength is renewed when we put our hope in Him because His strength never falters. We've talked about this before, but it's worth repeating: this doesn't always mean our circumstances get easier, but it's easier for us to navigate situations when we're resting and trusting in the Lord's strength, not our own.

Verse Breakdown

- Often said in scripture when referencing other scripture, specifically Old Testament law

Isaiah is speaking to Israel, prophecying what's to come. Israel would know The Law (Genesis-Deuteronomy).

"Do you not know? Have you not heard? The Lord is the everlasting God, the Creator of the whole earth. He never becomes faint or weary; there is no limit to his understanding."

attributes of God

Isaiah 40:28 CSB

When we choose to listen and we put our hope in Him, He renews us in a way nothing else can. His strength NEVER fades!

- "Have you not heard" becomes more than a simple question. There are countless examples of the Lord's power, strength, & sovereignty in the law. If someone had not heard, it was because they chose not to listen.

Your turn! Turn the page and use the margins provided to break down Scripture for yourself.

Once you've completed the "Reflect" section, come back and make a note of how you can apply this Scripture to your life and/or how you should respond to the Lord in light of what you've observed.

_____
_____
_____

Other Scriptures to consider
ROMANS 8:26–30 | LUKE 12:25–28 | II CORINTHIANS 12:1–10

Isaiah 40:21-31 (NIV)

HEAVENLY STRENGTH AND COMFORT

Do you not know? Have you not heard? Has it not been told you from the beginning? Have you not understood since the earth was founded? He sits enthroned above the circle of the earth, and its people are like grasshoppers. He stretches out the heavens like a canopy, and spreads them out like a tent to live in. He brings princes to naught and reduces the rulers of this world to nothing. No sooner are they planted, no sooner are they sown, no sooner do they take root in the ground, than He blows on them and they wither, and a whirlwind sweeps them away like chaff. "To whom will you compare Me? Or who is My equal?" says the Holy One. Lift up your eyes and look to the heavens: Who created all these? He who brings out the starry host one by one and calls forth each of them by name. Because of His great power and mighty strength, not one of them is missing. Why do you complain, Jacob?

Why do you say, Israel, "My way is hidden from the Lord; my cause is disregarded by my God"? Do you not know? Have you not heard? The Lord is the everlasting God, the Creator of the ends of the earth. He will not grow tired or weary, and His understanding no one can fathom. He gives strength to the weary and increases the power of the weak. Even youths grow tired and weary, and young men stumble and fall; but those who hope in the Lord will renew their strength. They will soar on wings like eagles; they will run and not grow weary, they will walk and not be faint.

Reflect

Who is the author of this passage? Who is the audience?

How do you think this passage impacted the audience?

Reflect

What do you see about the Lord?

What key themes do you see?

DAY 18

There is but one Lord,
Jesus Christ, through whom all things
came and through whom we live.

I CORINTHIANS 8:6 NIV

Doing What We Know

Today may be a little challenging. We're going to talk about some Old Testament history, and the call to action may be something you have to really think through. I think, at this point, you're ready for it, though, so let's dig in.

In the Old Testament, the Lord gave Israel very specific rules. There were rules for living in order to make sure Israel stayed healthy and strong. There were rules for eating, relationships, and sanitation. Some of the most repeated rules, however, had to do with sacrifices and idols. These laws strictly prohibited people from eating anything that was sacrificed to idols. God's number one rule was to worship only Him, so food sacrificed to any other god was considered unclean.

When Jesus died and resurrected, the Old Testament rules (also known as Mosaic law) were fulfilled because Jesus was the final sacrifice for sin and conquered death. This is the gospel, and it truly is the good news. But in practice, this was hard for many people to grasp. They grew up following these laws, and suddenly, they weren't required to follow them anymore. Some people still felt guilt for eating food that was sacrificed to idols, even though that law no longer bound them.

This is an incredibly complex issue because there are so many different things we could talk about here, especially if we continue through all of II Corinthians chapter 8. However, I want to focus on the first verse because it's so relevant to culture today: "Knowledge puffs up while love builds up."

In the early church, people knew the old law, but their knowledge of the old law and the fulfillment of it were pointless if they didn't change their ways to reflect their knowledge. Similarly, we often rely on knowledge to tell people our position on something, specifically with Scripture. We recite verses and quotes from theologians thinking it's enough to show we love God, but the truth is that knowledge without action means nothing. Just because we know the Bible, know how to study the Bible, and know about God doesn't mean we automatically love Him or love others like He does. In fact, if knowing about God is more important to us than loving like Him, we're walking the line of knowledge becoming an idol.

To be honest, I have wrestled with this myself. I crave knowledge and love learning the Bible, but when I studied this passage, I wondered if I show the love of God and put what I learn into practice as much as I read and study. Many times, the answer has been no, which is hard to admit.

Here's the takeaway: when knowledge is more important than action, we've missed the point entirely. Yes, it's important to know the Bible and to be able to discern what's true from what's false. *But,* why not love like Jesus first? We will always be learning while we study Scripture. In fact, that's one of my favorite things about it! But we can't wait until we know everything to start putting into practice what we do know. Let's put our knowledge to work now and start living out the love we know!

I Corinthians 8:1-6 (NIV)

DOING WHAT WE KNOW

Now about food sacrificed to idols: We know that "We all possess knowledge." But knowledge puffs up while love builds up. Those who think they know something do not yet know as they ought to know. But whoever loves God is known by God. So then, about eating food sacrificed to idols: We know that "An idol is nothing at all in the world" and that "There is no God but one." For even if there are so-called gods, whether in heaven or on earth (as indeed there are many "gods" and many "lords"), yet for us there is but one God, the Father, from whom all things came and for whom we live; and there is but one Lord, Jesus Christ, through whom all things came and through whom we live.

Reflect

Who is the author of this passage? Who is the audience?

How do you think this passage impacted the audience?

Reflect

What do you see about the Lord?

What key themes do you see?

Verse Breakdown

- **Context:** Paul is talking to the Corinthians about questions they've had regarding what is & isn't allowed.

- Paul refocuses the question.

- Head knowledge is important, but it leaves room for pride.

- Instead of focusing on rules, we ought to focus on how we can best show love to our brothers & sisters in Christ.

"Now about food sacrificed to idols: We know that "We all possess knowledge." But knowledge puffs up while love builds up."

1 Corinthians 8:1
NIV

- Anyone can learn something. In this case, anyone could have head knowledge about rules.

- *This verse is important to understand as the rest of the chapter is studied.

In light of what you learned and observed, how can you apply this to your life and/or how should you respond to the Lord?

_____
_____
_____
_____
_____

Other Scriptures to consider
JAMES 1:19-27 | JOHN 15:1-17 | ROMANS 7:4

DAY 19

Because of the Lord's faithful love we do not perish, for His mercies never end. They are new every morning; great is Your faithfulness!

LAMENTATIONS 3:22–24 CSB

Hope in His Faithfulness

Today's passage is short, but it is so profound. At first glance, it doesn't seem that way. It reads like a psalm, offering encouragement and praise to the Lord. This passage is profound, however, because of when it was written. Lamentations was written by the prophet Jeremiah. He was a prophet of the Lord before and during the capture of the exiles of Israel and Judah.

To give a quick synopsis: The nation of Israel split into two nations, Israel and Judah. Over time, both nations turned away from the Lord as a result of wicked kings. For years, the Lord sent different prophets to warn the nations that they would be conquered if they continued in their sin. Since I just told you Jeremiah was a prophet during exile, you can guess how the story played out.

Israel and Judah were conquered by outside nations and sent into exile. The first two chapters of Lamentations (which I encourage you to read before really digging into today's entry) give good insight into how far Israel and Judah fell. Jeremiah spent years pleading with God's people to turn from sin. In return he was mocked, beaten, and imprisoned. His writing of Lamentations is a lament for the people of God. He was grieving everything they had lost and everything he went through.

Even still, he remembered God. He remembered that God's love is faithful. He remembered that the Lord is just. He remembered that the Lord doesn't give up on His people. I'm sure it felt as though He had forgotten about them at the time, but we know He didn't because a few hundred years later, He sent the Messiah to save them and the whole world.

We read story after story in the Bible about everything God has done, but somehow, when we're in the thick of life, we think His goodness and faithfulness stop with our circumstances. Friend, that's not the case at all! We have hope in all circumstances because God's faithful love is on display for us regularly. We see it in His Word, and we see it in the lives of those around us. Don't ever let the enemy trick you into believing His mercies stop with you. They are new every morning, and He is where our hope is!

Lamentations 3:19–24 (CSB)
HOPE IN HIS FAITHFULNESS

Remember my affliction and my homelessness, the wormwood and the poison. I continually remember them and have become depressed. Yet I call this to mind, and therefore I have hope: Because of the Lord's faithful love we do not perish, for His mercies never end. They are new every morning; great is Your faithfulness! I say, "The Lord is my portion, therefore I will put my hope in Him."

Reflect

Who is the author of this passage? Who is the audience?

How do you think this passage impacted the audience?

Reflect

What do you see about the Lord?

What key themes do you see?

Verse Breakdown

[The context of this verse brings it alive. Jeremiah had unsuccessfully warned Israel of its exile due to their sin. He was imprisoned & humiliated as he warned Israel but they refused to listen & Jeremiah was witnessing the consequences of their actions.
↳ Devastation, total conquering]

● A share of something - in this case, Jeremiah made a point to say the Lord was his portion

● Jeremiah

"I say, 'The Lord is my portion, therefore I will put my hope in him.'"

● What is it there for?

Lamentations 3:24
CSB

● Many may put their hope in things or circumstances. If you put your hope in the Lord, you see that hope in anything else is fruitless.

Remember, Jeremiah spent previous chapters lamenting the absolute devastation of Israel, BUT he is able to worship & give thanks to God because he knows that God is greater than any situation or circumstance!

In light of what you learned and observed, how can you apply this to your life and/or how should you respond to the Lord?

_____
_____
_____
_____
_____

Other Scriptures to consider
LAMENTATION 1-2 | PSALM 25 | JOHN 1:9-18

DAY 20

Cast all your anxiety on Him because He cares for you.

I PETER 5:7 NIV

Embracing Humility

I think many of us have heard I Peter 5:7: "Cast all your anxiety on Him because He cares for you." It's such an encouraging verse, and it expresses the same beautiful message we see in other passages. I love this verse in this specific context, though, because it really speaks to our nature.

Peter is calling the church to humility. We don't like to be humble. If we have something cool, we want to show it off. If we have authority, we like to make it known. Maybe we're not abrasive about it, but we like to feel special and important. Obviously, these attitudes are not Christlike, and if we're honest, we'll admit that humility doesn't come naturally to us.

I have a young daughter, and I often tell her to pick up her playroom or put away her laundry. She's five years old, and I know she can put her laundry away on her own. I know she is capable of sorting her clothes and putting them in the correct drawers. I also know, however, that her attention span isn't long and that she hasn't quite developed the skills necessary to do things that need to get done just because they need to get done. Because I love her and know what she is capable of, I often step in to help. I tell her what steps need to be taken to complete the task. I remind her that we have to do laundry because we need to have clean clothes. I tell her that we fold things and put them away nicely because we need to take care of what God has blessed us with.

God works in a similar way with us. He knows humility goes against our nature. The way I make it clear to my daughter that she needs to put her clothes away, He makes it clear that He opposes the proud. He doesn't just tell us to be humble and leave us to our own devices to make that happen, though. He walks in that discomfort with us; He says we can cast our cares on Him. Like my encouragement and help with a five-year-old's laundry, God cares for us enough to help us fulfill the commands He gives us.

I don't know about you, but knowing that God gives us everything we need to do what He asks of us gives me a much deeper insight into how much God loves me and how far He will go to pursue me.

Verse Breakdown

- Don't forget: we are not in charge, and we are not the main character.

- The Lord is mighty, the Lord is the one in control, & everything is for His glory.

"Humble yourselves, therefore, under the mighty hand of God, so that he may exalt you at the proper time, casting all your cares on him, because he cares about you."

- His timing is perfect.

- A sense of urgency, to throw.

1 Peter 5:6-7
CSB

- A beautiful truth!

verse 7 is an incredible source of encouragment, but let us remember to be humble, obedient, and trust the Lord's sovereignty and perfect timing in every circumstance.

Your turn! Turn the page and use the margins provided to break down Scripture for yourself.

Once you've completed the "Reflect" section, come back and make a note of how you can apply this Scripture to your life and/or how you should respond to the Lord in light of what you've observed.

_____
_____
_____
_____
_____

Other Scriptures to consider
LUKE 14:7-14 | JAMES 4 | MICAH 6:8

I Peter 5:1-11 (NIV)
EMBRACING HUMILITY

To the elders among you, I appeal as a fellow elder and a witness of Christ's sufferings who also will share in the glory to be revealed: Be shepherds of God's flock that is under your care, watching over them—not because you must, but because you are willing, as God wants you to be; not pursuing dishonest gain, but eager to serve; not lording it over those entrusted to you, but being examples to the flock. And when the Chief Shepherd appears, you will receive the crown of glory that will never fade away. In the same way, you who are younger, submit yourselves to your elders. All of you, clothe yourselves with humility toward one another, because, "God opposes the proud but shows favor to the humble." Humble yourselves, therefore, under God's mighty hand, that He may lift you up in due time. Cast all your anxiety on Him because He cares for you. Be alert and of sober mind. Your enemy the devil prowls around like a roaring lion looking for someone to devour. Resist him, standing firm in the faith, because you know that the family of believers throughout the world is undergoing the same kind of sufferings. And the God of all grace, who called you to His eternal glory in Christ, after you have suffered a little while, will Himself restore you and make you strong, firm and steadfast. To Him be the power for ever and ever. Amen.

Reflect

Who is the author of this passage? Who is the audience?

How do you think this passage impacted the audience?

Reflect

What do you see about the Lord?

What key themes do you see?

DAY 21

Then Moses and the Israelites sang
this song to the LORD. They said:
The LORD is my strength and my song;
He has become my salvation.

EXODUS 15:1–2 CSB

The Power of God

Aside from Jesus, Moses is arguably one of the most important people in the Bible, but Moses had a rocky start. In Sunday school, many of us learn how Moses was hidden among reeds in the Nile River in a basket, adopted by Pharaoh's daughter, raised as Egyptian royalty, then ended up leading Israel out of captivity after ten plagues. What we don't hear much about are Moses's failures.

Moses was a murderer and a coward. He killed an Egyptian and then ran away when he realized he couldn't hide what he had done. When God spoke to him from the burning bush, Moses came up with excuse after excuse as to why he couldn't lead Israel out of Egypt. It wasn't until God grew angry that Moses started to obey, and even then, Moses wasn't perfect. Regardless, the Lord used Moses in a way He didn't use anyone else. Moses was chosen to lead God's people to the promised land. Moses, the man who ran away from consequences and made excuses, was one of the only men to meet the Lord face to face. He knew God as a man knows a friend (Exodus 33:11). He spent time with Him. He stood in the presence of God's glory.

In this passage, we learn how Moses transformed from being a coward to a man who loved, followed, and revered the Lord. A couple of things stand out to me here. First, how awesome is our God? Who is like Him? This passage describes the might and power of God, and it's awe-inspiring. Second, the same God who split the seas is the God who fights for us today! He knows you. He loves you. And just like He transformed the life of Moses, He is transforming each of us. He is our strength, our song, and our salvation.

For deeper insight into this Scripture, I encourage you to read Exodus 14. It's here where we see Pharaoh change his mind and pursue Israel after allowing them to leave. When we see today's passage in light of chapter 14, it gives us a better understanding of what Israel went through and how Moses was feeling as he sang this song.

Exodus 15:1–13 (CSB)

THE POWER OF GOD

Then Moses and the Israelites sang this song to the Lord. They said:

I will sing to the Lord, for He is highly exalted; He has thrown the horse and its rider into the sea.

The Lord is my strength and my song; He has become my salvation. This is my God, and I will praise Him, my father's God, and I will exalt Him. The Lord is a warrior; the Lord is His name. He threw Pharaoh's chariots and his army into the sea; the elite of his officers were drowned in the Red Sea. The floods covered them; they sank to the depths like a stone. Lord, Your right hand is glorious in power.

Lord, Your right hand shattered the enemy. You overthrew Your adversaries by Your great majesty.

You unleashed your burning wrath; it consumed them like stubble. The water heaped up at the blast from Your nostrils; the currents stood firm like a dam. The watery depths congealed in the heart of the sea. The enemy said: "I will pursue, I will overtake, I will divide the spoil. My desire will be gratified at their expense. I will draw my sword; my hand will destroy them." But You blew with your breath, and the sea covered them. They sank like lead in the mighty waters. LORD, who is like You among the gods? Who is like You, glorious in holiness, revered with praises, performing wonders? You stretched out Your right hand, and the earth swallowed them. With Your faithful love, You will lead the people You have redeemed; You will guide them to Your holy dwelling with Your strength.

Reflect

Who is the author of this passage? Who is the audience?

How do you think this passage impacted the audience?

Reflect

What do you see about the Lord?

_____
_____
_____
_____
_____
_____
_____
_____
_____
_____
_____
_____

What key themes do you see?

_____
_____
_____
_____
_____
_____
_____
_____
_____
_____
_____
_____

Verse Breakdown

> *Context makes this text so much richer! CH 14 details Israel's exodus from Egypt & the parting of the Red Sea.

interesting because Moses wasn't really enslaved. His salvation looked different from the rest of Israel's.

"The Lord is my strength and my song; he has become my salvation. This is my God, and I will praise him, my father's God, and I will exalt him."

The Lord's grace & salvation should prompt us to worship!

Exodus 15:2 CSB

The Lord is in the business of redemption. There is no one too far gone. Moses was a murderer & Israel often doubted the Lord, but He redeemed them anyway.

Not the gods of Egypt that had surrounded Israel as they were enslaved. The LORD was their God.

In light of what you learned and observed, how can you apply this to your life and/or how should you respond to the Lord?

_____
_____
_____
_____
_____

Other Scriptures to consider
EXODUS 14 | PSALM 91 | PSALM 106

DAY 22

There was a man sent from God whose name was John. He came as a witness to testify concerning that light, so that through him all might believe. He himself was not the light; he came only as a witness to the light.

JOHN 1:6–8 NIV

Our Light in the Darkness

It can be hard to study Scripture. The Bible isn't always a page turner. Some things are complex to read, and other things are even more complex to understand. If I'm being honest, I find the Gospel of John to be one of the hardest books of the Bible to read. There's a lot of complex imagery and metaphorical writing. The Gospel of John is hard for me to get through, but it's also one of the most beautiful books in the Bible. The Gospels each give an account of Jesus's life from a different perspective, and John shows us the life of Jesus as the Son of God. As hard as it is for me to break down much of the text, the truth in the gospel is so powerful.

In the beginning was the Word. The Word was with God. The Word was God. Jesus was fully man but also fully God, and He doesn't just appear in the New Testament. He was with God in the beginning. We see this in Genesis when God says, "Let Us make man in Our image" (Genesis 1:26 CSB, emphasis added).

Friend, this verse is at the beginning of the Bible and points us to Jesus! As you study the Old Testament, you may start to notice appearances of Jesus the Son of God throughout different stories. This is such an encouragement to me!

The promises of God are redemptive, and the redemption story started at the beginning. From complete darkness and void, God created life. He spoke and brought light to the darkness. In the darkness of our lives, Christ is the light, and the darkness—our sin—cannot overcome Him. He conquered death, and He conquered our sin. We may feel overwhelmed by dark circumstances, but we can rest knowing that God speaks light into every dark place and secures our victory! We aren't designed to live in sin and struggle. Many times our struggles come from our sinful nature, but the Lord sent His Son to save us from that. This doesn't mean we won't experience hard things. We live in a fallen and broken world that experiences times of suffering and sorrow as a result of sin. We can rejoice, however, knowing that Jesus has conquered sin and that ultimately the Lord has the victory over every single struggle and hardship we face.

Verse Breakdown

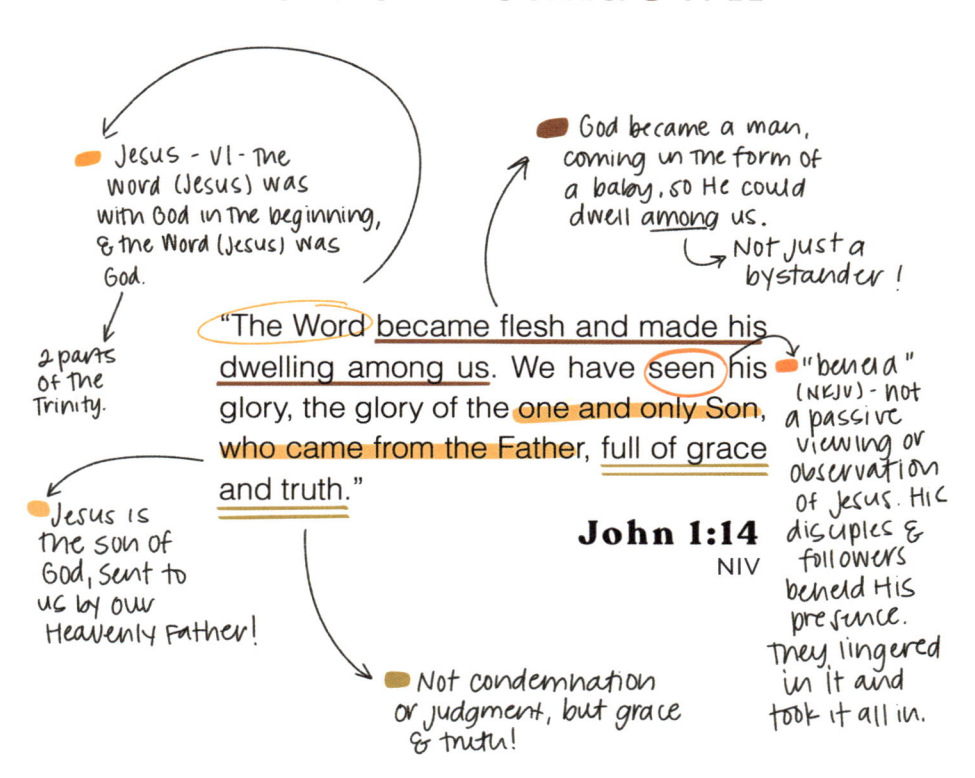

- Jesus - v1 - The Word (Jesus) was with God in the beginning, & the Word (Jesus) was God.

- 2 parts of the Trinity.

- God became a man, coming in the form of a baby, so He could dwell among us.
  ↳ Not just a bystander!

> "The Word became flesh and made his dwelling among us. We have seen his glory, the glory of the one and only Son, who came from the Father, full of grace and truth."
>
> **John 1:14** NIV

- Jesus is the Son of God, sent to us by our Heavenly Father!

- "beheld" (NKJV) - not a passive viewing or observation of Jesus. His disciples & followers beheld His presence. They lingered in it and took it all in.

- Not condemnation or judgment, but grace & truth!

Your turn! Turn the page and use the margins provided to break down Scripture for yourself.

Once you've completed the "Reflect" section, come back and make a note of how you can apply this Scripture to your life and/or how you should respond to the Lord in light of what you've observed.

___
___
___
___
___

Other Scriptures to consider
GENESIS 1:26 | GENESIS 3:14-15 | JOHN 3:13-31

John 1:1–14 (NIV)

OUR LIGHT IN THE DARKNESS

In the beginning was the Word, and the Word was with God, and the Word was God. He was with God in the beginning. Through Him all things were made; without Him nothing was made that has been made. In Him was life, and that life was the light of all mankind. The light shines in the darkness, and the darkness has not overcome it. There was a man sent from God whose name was John. He came as a witness to testify concerning that light, so that through him all might believe. He himself was not the light; he came only as a witness to the light.

The true light that gives light to everyone was coming into the world. He was in the world, and though the world was made through Him, the world did not recognize Him. He came to that which was His own, but His own did not receive Him. Yet to all who did receive Him, to those who believed in His name, He gave the right to become children of God—children born not of natural descent, nor of human decision or a husband's will, but born of God. The Word became flesh and made His dwelling among us. We have seen His glory, the glory of the one and only Son, who came from the Father, full of grace and truth.

Reflect

Who is the author of this passage? Who is the audience?

How do you think this passage impacted the audience?

Reflect

What do you see about the Lord?

What key themes do you see?

DAY 23

The LORD is close to the brokenhearted
and saves those who are crushed in spirit.

PSALM 34:18 NIV

Delivered from Many Troubles

Recently, I grieved the loss of two people I loved dearly—my grandfather and a close friend. The loss of my grandfather was somewhat expected, but we didn't get a lot of closure, so I was still processing his death when my friend died unexpectedly two weeks later. I knew her from church, and she served our production team faithfully. She volunteered for almost every service, which meant she would hear the same sermon multiple times on any given weekend; still, during every service she would be so attentive and engaged you would think she had never heard it before. She loved the Lord with her whole heart, and everyone who talked to her ended up learning about Jesus. She was bold, selfless, and faithful. And then she was suddenly gone, and I was angry. I couldn't understand why God would let her die when she served Him so faithfully.

In the wake of those losses, in an effort to find comfort, I spent a lot of time in Psalm 34. Whenever it felt like things were too heavy and everything was too much, I remembered this passage.

"The Lord is close to the brokenhearted and saves those who are crushed in spirit. The righteous person may have many troubles, but the Lord delivers him from them all" (Psalm 34:18–19 NIV).

The last thing my friend said on social media was, "I am not afraid to die, and I trust Him with my whole heart." When I realized that she was in the presence of the One she loved and trusted with her whole heart, the sting of her death slightly subsided. These verses were a balm to my hurting soul. They reminded me that God is not far off. They reminded me that while troubles on this earth are certain, the Lord has victory over all of them.

Psalm 34:15–22 (NIV)

DELIVERED FROM MANY TROUBLES

The eyes of the LORD are on the righteous, and His ears are attentive to their cry; but the face of the LORD is against those who do evil, to blot out their name from the earth. The righteous cry out, and the LORD hears them; He delivers them from all their troubles. The LORD is close to the brokenhearted and saves those who are crushed in spirit. The righteous person may have many troubles, but the LORD delivers him from them all; He protects all his bones, not one of them will be broken. Evil will slay the wicked; the foes of the righteous will be condemned. The

Lord will rescue His servants; no one who takes refuge in Him will be condemned.

Reflect

Who is the author of this passage? Who is the audience?

How do you think this passage impacted the audience?

Reflect

What do you see about the Lord?

What key themes do you see?

Verse Breakdown

This verse is such a comfort to me!

- The Lord is not distant! He is close to us. He does not forget us.

"**The Lord is close to the brokenhearted** and (saves) those who are crushed in spirit."

Psalm 34:18
NIV

- "saves" doesn't always look the way we think or want, but that doesn't mean He is distant. Remember, He is sovereign & sees the whole picture!

- When the world & life circumstances knock us down & crush our spirits, we can rest knowing He is with us!

In light of what you learned and observed, how can you apply this to your life and/or how should you respond to the Lord?

Other Scriptures to consider
PSALM 147 | JOHN 19:28-37 | REVELATION 7:11-17

DAY 24

For God so loved the world that He gave His one and only Son, that whoever believes in Him shall not perish but have eternal life.

JOHN 3:16 NIV

"There is no condemnation for those who are in Christ."
Romans 8:1

Salvation, Not Condemnation

John 3:16 is probably the most famous Bible verse. It's often the first verse we memorize because it's the gospel in a sentence. What I love about this passage, outside of the gospel message, is the context. In this passage, Jesus is talking to a man named Nicodemus who was a member of the Sanhedrin. The Sanhedrin was a group of religious leaders, many of them Pharisees, that came together to make decisions and uphold the religious law. They were high-ranking and laser focused on making sure the Mosaic law was followed, so it makes sense that when Jesus came and taught a new law (grace), they weren't too happy about it. The Pharisees became even more unhappy when people started following Jesus rather than following the law that gave them authority. Eventually, the Pharisees had Jesus executed because of their jealousy and zeal for the law. Nicodemus was a Pharisee, and because of his affiliation, he had this secret conversation with Jesus at night. Nicodemus had some pressing questions to ask Jesus.

We only see Nicodemus twice more in Scripture. In one instance, he plays devil's advocate as a way to stand up for Jesus without making it obvious that he follows Him. In the last instance, he and another man remove Jesus's body from the cross. The gospel is explained in these few verses in John, but the life-changing transformation of the gospel is seen in the life of the man Jesus spoke to: Nicodemus went from meeting with Christ in secret to helping prepare Jesus's body for burial. He went from having questions and being scared of what his peers would think to publicly laying Him in a tomb. Only the gospel has this kind of power!

As we navigate our day-to-day lives, let's remember that the gospel is life-saving and life-changing. Scripture is clear—Jesus came to earth and died so that we could have salvation. He didn't come to condemn us but to give us life!

Verse Breakdown

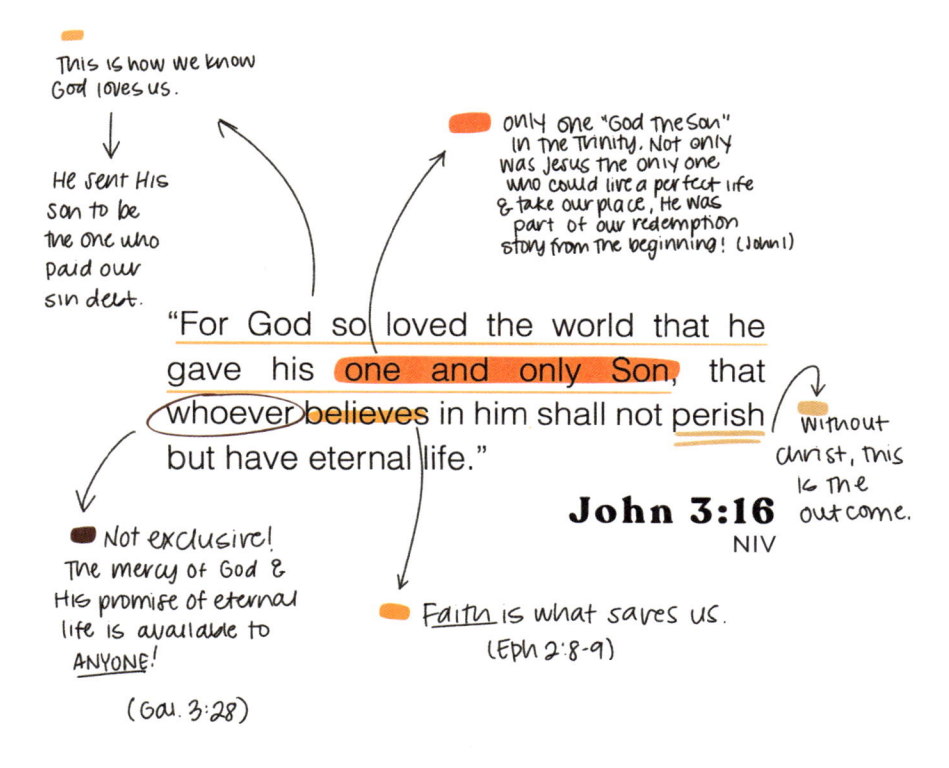

This is how we know God loves us.
↓
He sent His Son to be the one who paid our sin debt.

Only one "God The Son" in the Trinity. Not only was Jesus the only one who could live a perfect life & take our place, He was part of our redemption story from the beginning! (John 1)

"For God so loved the world that he gave his **one and only Son**, that whoever believes in him shall not perish but have eternal life."

John 3:16
NIV

Without Christ, this is the outcome.

Not exclusive! The mercy of God & His promise of eternal life is available to ANYONE!
(Gal. 3:28)

Faith is what saves us. (Eph 2:8-9)

Your turn! Turn the page and use the margins provided to break down Scripture for yourself.

Once you've completed the "Reflect" section, come back and make a note of how you can apply this Scripture to your life and/or how you should respond to the Lord in light of what you've observed.

_____
_____
_____
_____
_____
_____

John 3:13–17 (NIV)

SALVATION, NOT CONDEMNATION

No one has ever gone into heaven except the one who came from heaven—the Son of Man. Just as Moses lifted up the snake in the wilderness, so the Son of Man must be lifted up, that everyone who believes may have eternal life in Him. For God so loved the world that He gave His one and only Son, that whoever believes in Him shall not perish but have eternal life. For God did not send His Son into the world to condemn the world, but to save the world through Him. The true light that gives light to everyone was coming into the world. He was in the world, and though the world was made through Him, the world did not recognize Him. He came to that which was His own, but His own did not receive Him. Yet to all who did receive Him, to those who believed in His name, He gave the right to become children of God—children born not of natural descent, nor of human decision or a husband's will, but born of God. The Word became flesh and made His dwelling among us. We have seen His glory, the glory of the one and only Son, who came from the Father, full of grace and truth.

Other Scriptures to consider
ROMANS 8:1-4 | JOHN 5:24 | II CORINTHIANS 3:7-18
EXODUS 34:29-35

Reflect

Who is the author of this passage? Who is the audience?

How do you think this passage impacted the audience?

Reflect

What do you see about the Lord?

What key themes do you see?

DAY 25

Your hands made me and
formed me; give me understanding
to learn Your commands.

PSALM 119:73 NIV

Delighting in the Word

Psalm 119 is my favorite chapter of the Bible. The psalm is long—176 verses long. Psalm 119 is an acrostic psalm, which means that in the original language, the lines in each stanza followed an alphabetical pattern. To us, it would be like reading a poem where every line in the first stanza started with the letter A, every line in the second stanza would start with the letter B, and so on until Z. Not only is this psalm beautiful to read, but it's also an impressive piece of writing.

In Psalm 119, the psalmist writes of his love for the Word of God. He writes about how the Word teaches, encourages, and refines him. He talks about the comfort, hope, and lessons found in the Word. I love this stanza specifically because it reminds us of so many different things about the Lord. It reminds us that He is the Creator who intentionally formed us. It reminds us that He is righteous and that even in hard times, He is faithful.

It's also a call to action. It reminds us that obedience to the Lord is important and that we ought to reflect Him with our words and actions. It reminds us that meditation on His Word is a wellspring of life. Finally, it calls us to boldness—not to be ashamed of following Him and His Word.

As we close out our journey through Scripture, my prayer is that this psalm is a reminder that the Word of God is a gift. It's my prayer that over the last few weeks, your love for the Lord and His Word has grown to mirror the love the psalmist had for Scripture. I pray that you've not only started to understand how and why we study Scripture but also that your desire to study Scripture has grown. Finally, I pray that His statutes become the theme of your song (Psalm 119:54) and that you continue to grow closer to Him.

Psalm 119:73–80 (NIV)

DELIGHTING IN THE WORD

Your hands made me and formed me; give me understanding to learn Your commands. May those who fear You rejoice when they see me, for I have put my hope in Your word. I know, Lord, that Your laws are righteous, and that in faithfulness You have afflicted me. May Your unfailing love be my comfort, according to Your promise to Your servant. Let Your compassion come to me that I may live, for Your law is my delight. May the arrogant be put to shame for wronging me without cause; but I will meditate on Your precepts. May those who fear You turn to me, those who understand Your statutes. May I wholeheartedly follow Your decrees, that I may not be put to shame.

Reflect

Who is the author of this passage? Who is the audience?

How do you think this passage impacted the audience?

Reflect

What do you see about the Lord?

What key themes do you see?

Verse Breakdown

- This is a prayer to the Lord.

- The psalmist recognizes that he cannot wholeheartedly follow the Lord's word on his own.

- Not partially. Not lukewarm. The psalmist wants to follow the Lord & His word with his WHOLE heart.

> "May I wholeheartedly follow your decrees, that I may not be put to shame."
>
> **Psalm 119:80**
> NIV

- law, statutes, word.

- We ought to care about what others think about us in light of our relationship with God
  → How am I representing Him? Am I obedient to His word? Do I reflect His nature?

In light of what you learned and observed, how can you apply this to your life and/or how should you respond to the Lord?

_____
_____
_____
_____
_____
_____

Other Scriptures to consider
PSALM 147 | JOHN 19:28-37 | REVELATION 7:11-17

ABOUT THE AUTHOR

Carrie Cristancho

Carrie Cristancho, founder and owner of *True and Lovely Co.*, has a passion for the Word of God. Her desire is to share Christ, and creatively encourage Bible study and Biblical literacy through Bible journaling, Bible teaching, and providing resources. Carrie lives in Tennessee with her husband and daughter. She is a graphic designer, worship leader, and artist who loves to collect sneakers, watch old sitcoms, and host game nights.

DaySpring
LIVE YOUR FAITH

Dear Friend,

This Bible resource was prayerfully crafted with you in mind—it was thoughtfully written, designed, and packaged to encourage you right where you are. At DaySpring Bibles, our vision is to see every person experience the life-changing message of God's love, not just on Sundays, but every day of the week. As we worked through rough drafts, design changes, edits and details, we prayed for you to encounter His unfailing love and indescribable peace within the pages of this book. It is our hope that this resource doesn't only fill your head with knowledge, but strengthens your connection with and understanding of God.

THE DAYSPRING BIBLE TEAM

Additional copies of this book and
other DaySpring titles can be purchased
at fine retailers everywhere.
Order online at dayspring.com
or
by phone at 1-877-751-4347

Whatever is True & Lovely: Devotional Guide
Copyright © 2022 Carrie Cristancho, all rights reserved.
First Edition, May 2022

Published by:

DaySpring

21154 Highway 16 East
Siloam Springs, AR 72761
dayspring.com

All rights reserved. *Whatever is True & Lovely: Devotional Guide* is under copyright protection. No part of this book may be used or reproduced in any manner whatsoever without written permission except in the case of brief quotations embodied in critical articles and reviews.

Scripture quotations marked CSB®, are taken from the Christian Standard Bible®, Copyright © 2017 by Holman Bible Publishers. Used by permission. Christian Standard Bible®, and CSB® are federally registered trademarks of Holman Bible Publishers.

Scripture quotations marked ESV are taken from the ESV Bible® (The Holy Bible, English Standard Version®), copyright ©2001 by Crossway Bibles, a publishing ministry of Good News Publishers. Used by permission. All rights reserved.

Scripture quotations marked NIV are taken from the Holy Bible, New International Version®, NIV®. Copyright © 1973, 1978, 1984, 2011 by Biblica, Inc.® Used by permission of Zondervan. All rights reserved worldwide. www.zondervan.com. The "NIV" and "New International Version" are trademarks registered in the United States Patent and Trademark Office by Biblica, Inc.®

Written by: Carrie Cristancho
Cover Design by: Becca Barnett

Printed in United States
Prime: J7565
ISBN: 978-1-64870-438-3